*Praise for Howard Schultz
and Rajiv Chandrasekaran's*

For Love of Country

"This splendid book should be read by every American. It is a story of heroes, of sacrifice, of valor. But it is also a story of resilience, recovery, and a continuing desire to serve our country and its citizens. You must be made of stone to read this and not shed tears. But the book's message is that, after the tears, we must not forget the sacrifices those in uniform and their families have made for all of us over the last thirteen years; we must welcome back into our communities those who served not just with thanks and open arms, but with respect, admiration, and new lives and careers worthy of all they have done for all of us."   —Robert M. Gates, former secretary of defense and author of *Duty*

"These stories leave the reader with a profound sense of [our troops'] selfless service. . . . Schultz and Chandrasekaran never suggest that war is good. But the stories they tell are a welcome reminder of what soldiers have always known: that out of difficulty and trauma come a sense of spiritual self-worth and a dedication to the service of others."
—Maj. Gen. Robert H. Scales, *The Wall Street Journal*

"[Schultz and Chandrasekaran] are on target in calling for a societal salute to America's new generation of veterans."
—*St. Louis Post-Dispatch*

"A truly inspirational, uplifting book, one that will fill you with pride in America's new Greatest Generation in war and in peace."   —Gen. David H. Petraeus, U.S. Army, Retired

Howard Schultz

Howard Schultz is chairman and chief executive officer of Starbucks, where he has been recognized for his leadership, business ethics, and efforts to strengthen communities. He and his wife, Sheri, have pledged extensive support to help veterans make successful transitions to civilian life through the Schultz Family Foundation's Onward Veterans initiative. Schultz is the bestselling author of *Onward: How Starbucks Fought for Its Life Without Losing Its Soul* and *Pour Your Heart Into It*.

Rajiv Chandrasekaran

Rajiv Chandrasekaran is a former senior correspondent and associate editor at *The Washington Post*, where he worked from 1994 to 2015. He was the newspaper's bureau chief in Baghdad, Cairo, and Southeast Asia, and covered Afghanistan off and on for a decade. Chandrasekaran is the author of *Little America* and *Imperial Life in the Emerald City*, which was named one of the 10 Best Books of 2007 by *The New York Times*.

Also by Howard Schultz

Onward:
How Starbucks Fought for Its Life Without Losing Its Soul

Pour Your Heart Into It:
How Starbucks Built a Company One Cup at a Time

Also by Rajiv Chandrasekaran

Little America:
The War Within the War for Afghanistan

Imperial Life in the Emerald City:
Inside Iraq's Green Zone

 **For Love of Country**

FOR LOVE OF COUNTRY

WHAT OUR VETERANS

CAN TEACH US ABOUT

CITIZENSHIP, HEROISM,

AND SACRIFICE

Howard Schultz and
Rajiv Chandrasekaran

VINTAGE BOOKS
A Division of Penguin Random House LLC
New York

FIRST VINTAGE BOOKS EDITION, OCTOBER 2015

The Library of Congress has cataloged the Knopf edition as follows:
Schultz, Howard.
For love of country : what our veterans can teach us about citizenship, heroism, and sacrifice / Howard Schultz and Rajiv Chandrasekaran.
pages   cm
1. Iraq War, 2003–2011—Biography.
2. Afghan War, 2001—Biography.
3. Iraq War, 2003–2011—Veterans—United States.
4. Afghan War, 2001—Veterans—United States.
5. Veterans—United States—Biography.   6. Conduct of life.
I. Chandrasekaran, Rajiv.   II. Title.
DS79.766.A1S38 2014   956.7044'3092 DC23   [B]   2014030240

Vintage Books Trade Paperback ISBN: 978-1-101-87282-6
eBook ISBN: 978-1-101-87446-2

Author photograph © Fran Ramos-Sabugo Rodriguez
Interior art: American flag © charnsitr / Shutterstock;
American flag support ribbon © Adam Filipowicz/Shutterstock
Book design by Betty Lew

www.vintagebooks.com

Printed in the United States of America
10 9 8 7 6 5 4 3 2 1

For all those who served,

and for Sheri and Julie,

who share our gratitude for their courage and sacrifice.

Contents

 For Love of Country

Introduction

On Memorial Day 2008, Leroy Petry should have been asleep. He toiled on the night shift, as did most of his fellow Army Rangers. But that morning, as the sun beat down on his plywood hut, nervous energy throbbed through his veins, and he tossed in his bunk.

The evening before, Petry's commanders had received word that a senior al-Qaeda operative might be within striking distance of their forward operating base in the hills of eastern Afghanistan. Petry was on his eighth combat deployment, and he had performed more airborne assaults than he could remember, yet he treated each one like his first rodeo. He always brought extra food, double-checked his gear, and thought through contingency plans.

Finally, Petry gave up on sleep, rolled out of his bunk, and stumbled into his platoon's nearly empty tactical operations center. As he began to read his e-mail, he saw the watch officer nearby jolt upright. "Go wake everyone up," the officer barked.

Petry banged on doors and shook guys by their shoulders. Then he ran into the chow hall and grabbed a handful of beef jerky packets. When everyone assembled in the operations center, his restlessness was vindicated. He learned that his platoon would be heading out on a rare daylight mission to pursue the al-Qaeda operative.

After the briefing, he gathered his dozen-man squad of machine gunners. He knew they were concerned about swooping in at midday, when they couldn't rely on night-vision goggles to give them a distinct battlefield advantage. "You're on more even ground with them," warned Petry, a twenty-eight-year-old staff sergeant. "Be prepared for anything."

As a pair of dual-rotor Chinook helicopters ferried the platoon toward a remote cluster of homes where its target was believed to be hiding, Petry could see his own apprehension mirrored on the faces of his fellow Rangers. He hadn't been on a daylight raid in four years.

Shots were heard as soon as the helicopters landed and the Rangers hustled off the back ramp. While most of the Americans fired back and charged toward the buildings, Petry hung back with the platoon leader—their job was to command, not to kick down the doors themselves. As the Rangers started the search for their target, Petry heard over the radio that one of the squads had been delayed because it had initially entered the wrong building.

"I'm going to go with them," he told the platoon leader as he took off running. Along the way, he summoned Private First Class Lucas Robinson, a young member of the platoon, to join him.

Petry located the correct compound and stepped through a hole in the mud-brick wall that surrounded the outer courtyard, intending to catch up with the rest of the squad, which had already walked into a walled-off inner courtyard. As soon as he and Robinson entered, a burst of gunfire tore across the compound. Petry felt sharp pain in both of his thighs, but he mustered the strength to run toward a small outbuilding about twenty yards away, hoping its walls would provide protection from the gunmen, who had trained AK-47 rifles on the Rangers from a bunker at the far end of the courtyard. Robinson, who had been grazed on the side, followed behind.

As they crouched behind the building, Petry looked down at his legs. Blood seeped out of holes in each pant leg, but his bones felt intact, and no major blood vessels appeared to have been hit. *A flesh wound,* he thought. *I can keep fighting.*

Petry got on the radio to inform his platoon mates that he and Robinson had been shot. Then he pulled a thermobaric grenade from his vest and hurled it in the direction of the bunker. After it exploded, the incoming fire ceased.

At that moment, another Ranger, Sergeant Daniel Higgins, ran into the courtyard and joined Petry and Robinson next to the building. Higgins stood beside Robinson on one end of the ten-foot-long wall; Petry was on the other end, sitting on the dirt, peering around the corner. As Higgins inspected Robinson's wound, a grenade flew out of the bunker and landed ten yards from the Rangers. It detonated a second later, knocking Higgins and Robinson to the ground but leaving them unscathed.

"Keep your heads down," Petry called out.

Fearing that the insurgents would converge from both sides of the building and kill all three of them, he glanced around the corner again. He spotted two fighters in the bunker, both with ammunition clips strapped to their chests.

"Damn," Petry muttered to himself. *So much for my grenade.*

He turned to check on Robinson and Higgins. As he did, he saw an object land on the dirt a few feet from his comrades.

Another grenade, the size of a baseball, the color of an olive, with the texture of a pineapple, packing enough TNT to kill his buddies.

The others hadn't seen it. He knew that grenades typically have a four-and-a-half-second fuse. Even if he screamed out a warning, they wouldn't have time to move away. Both of them would die. So he lunged.

In the fraction of a second between observing the grenade and reaching for it, Petry, a father of four, expected to surrender his life.

"These are my brothers—family just like my wife and kids—and you protect the ones you love."

He grabbed the grenade with his right hand, lowered his head, and started to toss it away. As he let go, it exploded. The force of the blast propelled him backward and slammed him to the ground. He opened his eyes. *I guess I'm still alive.*

Then he caught sight of his right hand—or the place it had been. It appeared to have been cut off with a circular saw. He could see his radius and ulna, and a mass of flesh around his wrist. But no gushing blood.

Why isn't it spraying in the wind like in the movies?

He felt no pain.

Oh, crap, I guess I have to take care of this.

He reached down with his left hand, grabbed a tourniquet— all soldiers carried them—and cinched it around his right forearm. Then he looked over at Robinson and Higgins. They were staring in disbelief.

"Keep pulling security," Petry admonished. He wanted them scanning for insurgents, not looking at him.

At the sound of the explosion, the platoon's first sergeant ran into the compound. When he saw that Petry's hand was missing, he sought to pull the injured man to safety with a strap stitched to the back of his armored vest. "We're going to get you out of here."

"You're not taking me anywhere," Petry growled, "until we get those bastards."

He remained behind the wall, clutching his M4 carbine with his left hand. More soldiers stormed into the courtyard. As they began shooting at the bunker, a third gunman lurking in the other corner of the compound unleashed a volley of AK-47 rounds. One of them hit Specialist Christopher Gathercole in the face, just below his helmet, killing him.

It would take a few more hours and several dozen rounds of

ammunition, but the Rangers eventually killed all three insurgents. As the fighting dragged on, Petry hobbled over to the team's injury collection point.

"I need to take a look at you," the medic said.

"Start with the other guys," Petry replied. "I'm fine."

"No, you're not," he said, pointing to Petry's legs.

Petry looked down. His camouflage pants and boots were soaked in blood.

I want to keep fighting, but I guess my body is running out of juice.

As he was carried to a medical evacuation helicopter, Higgins hustled over to his side. He looked Petry in the eyes.

"You saved us, man."

HOWARD'S REFLECTIONS

Nearly five years later, in February 2013, I met Leroy Petry in a packed auditorium on the ninth floor of Starbucks' headquarters in Seattle. He was dressed in his Class A uniform, his left breast covered with multicolored ribbon bars, his arms decorated with gold chevrons identifying him as a sergeant first class. It was an Army uniform similar to those worn by so many other Americans who have served on multiple combat deployments—with one key difference: a five-pointed gold star hung from a light blue ribbon around his neck.

It was the Medal of Honor, our nation's highest award for combat valor.

Petry had been presented with the medal eighteen months earlier, after a thorough examination by Pentagon officials that included detailed interviews with Higgins, Robinson, and other Rangers who participated in the raid. Petry became just the second living recipient of the award since the Vietnam War.

"Every human impulse would tell someone to turn away. Every soldier is trained to seek cover. That's what Sergeant Leroy Petry could have done. Instead, this wounded Ranger, this twenty-eight-year-old man with his whole life ahead of him, this husband and father of four, did something extraordinary," President Obama said at a White House ceremony. His selfless act, the president said, "is the stuff of which heroes are made. This is the strength, the devotion that makes our troops the pride of every American."

The Starbucks Armed Forces Network, a group of our employees who have served in the military, had invited Petry to speak to us. As he shared his story, I found myself transfixed and humbled. Tears welled in my eyes. Here was a man brave enough to assume the ultimate risk so that others could live, and yet he spoke of himself only grudgingly, with the utmost modesty. He wanted the spotlight to fall on his brothers and sisters in uniform. "To be singled out is humbling," he told us. "But I consider every service member to be our heroes."

Petry's act that day in May 2008 might have been unique, but the values, courage, and dedication he embodies are universal among those Americans who have raised their right hand and sworn to defend our nation. I saw it in my father, who had been an Army medic during World War II, serving in the South Pacific, where he contracted yellow fever and malaria. I saw it in my high school friends who went off to fight in Vietnam. (My draft number was not among those ordered to boot camp.) And I have seen it in this generation of men and women at West Point, during a daylong visit the week after Navy SEALs killed Osama bin Laden.

I had been asked by Bill Campbell, a former longtime Apple computer board member, to address the academy's Black and Gold Forum, which invites business and government leaders to speak to the cadets about leadership. Arriving in the morning with my wife, Sheri, and son, Jordan, I immediately felt as if we were on sacred ground. We learned about the school's history, traditions, and emphasis on creating a remarkable cadre of young leaders, some of whom will spend their careers in the Army, becoming colonels and generals, others of whom will follow the path of many fellow graduates and ascend in the worlds of business and government service. Watching these cadets, in their crisp gray uniforms, saluting each other as they walked along the grounds, filled me with deep pride. In an era when many wonder if our nation has lost its way, West Point represents all that is still good about the United States.

John Culver, a senior member of the Starbucks executive leadership team, joined my family and me. I had invited him because he had Army blue in his blood. His late father, a full-bird colonel, had spent twenty-eight years in the service, including three combat tours in Vietnam. As John gazed upon the Plain, the hallowed parade field, through a window in the superintendent's office, he thought of his father and of the words General Douglas MacArthur famously intoned at the academy: "Duty, honor, country." And he began to cry.

When it came time for me to speak to the cadets, I, too, choked up. What I had absorbed in the preceding hours exceeded anything I could possibly impart to them. "It would be ill-advised for me to share any lessons of leadership with you," I told them. "It is I who should be learning from you. You are the true leaders." Then I moved quickly to a question-and-answer session.

My visit revealed to me just how disconnected I had been from these fellow citizens who have dedicated years of their lives to defending the freedom I hold dear. No one in my family or my circle of friends was serving in the armed forces. I had never visited a military base. Before going to West Point, I had never even spoken to anyone in uniform. As I look back, I'm embarrassed.

A few months later, a mutual friend put me in contact with Robert Gates, one of our country's most distinguished public servants,

who had just moved back to Washington State after serving as secretary of defense for four and a half years. I had been inspired by
his love for the troops, his ability to bridge partisan infighting inside
the Beltway, and his no-nonsense approach to leadership. At West
Point earlier that year, he famously warned that "any future defense
secretary who advises the president to again send a big American
land army into Asia or into the Middle East or Africa should have
his head examined, as General MacArthur so delicately put it."

He graciously accepted my invitation to visit our offices.
I meant to acquaint him with our company—I already knew he
loved our coffee—and invite him to join our board of directors.
But when he arrived, I was far more interested in hearing him talk
about our troops and his management of the wars than I was in
discussing corporate strategy. Over the next ninety minutes, he con-
veyed his adoration for those who served under him so movingly
that I wanted to jump in my car, drive an hour south to Joint Base
Lewis-McChord, and express my gratitude to as many people there
as I could.

But he also shared his grave concerns about the challenges our
troops face in their transition into civilian life: writing résumés that
make sense to people who don't work on bases, acquiring the skills
necessary to land a decent job, finding employers who value all
they've learned in the military. Disproportionate attention by the
media to the small number of veterans who have committed crimes,
or the minority of them who have returned home with serious mental and physical ailments, compared with those who have found
personal and professional success, or are charting a course toward
it, risks stigmatizing them.

War, Gates noted, unquestionably changes a person. "But it
doesn't mean it makes you dysfunctional," he told me. "Our veterans are loyal, easily trained, accustomed to being members of a

team—and they're mature. They have a foundation of character and experience that any business would want to build upon."

Getting to know Gates made me want to meet some of those troops for whom he cared so profoundly, so I did what I should have done years earlier: My wife and I drove down to Lewis-McChord, one of the largest military installations in the country and home to about forty-five thousand personnel. We met with dozens of soldiers. As they showed us around the base and took us for a ride in a Stryker armored vehicle, I asked them the most basic of questions: Why did you join? What was it like going to war? Some did so because they needed to pay bills or earn money for college. Others wanted to follow family tradition. But all of the soldiers I met, regardless of their reason for enlisting, were motivated by patriotism, by a calling to serve. *Why did it take me all this time to visit?* I thought as I headed back to my office. *I've lived here for thirty-three years.*

Gates's wise counsel—informally and as a member of our board—and my interactions with Starbucks employees who are veterans propelled us to commit in November 2013 to hire ten thousand veterans and active military spouses over the following five years. Gates joined me, along with Sergeant Petry, leaders from Lewis-McChord, and members of Washington State's congressional delegation, for the announcement at our headquarters. Addressing them and scores of our partners, I emphasized that our decision was not rooted in charity. "This is good business," I said. "We're going to hire the best and the brightest." Our company's culture would benefit, I told them, as our partners worked side by side with people who have defended our country and "done things that you can't even imagine."

In the run-up to the jobs event, Gates had introduced me to another awe-inspiring military leader, retired general Peter Chiarelli, the former vice chief of staff of the Army, who also had moved to Washington State from the other Washington. In much the same way that Gates had single-handedly propelled the Pentagon bureaucracy to more quickly deploy mine-resistant trucks to our troops in Iraq and Afghanistan, Chiarelli had led the charge to transform the military's approach to brain injuries and mental health care. He had sought to reduce the shockingly high rate of military suicides, in part by expanding initiatives to diagnose and treat post-traumatic stress.

Chiarelli knew the only way to begin to grasp the enormous health-care needs of this generation of veterans, and the incredible resiliency of many of those who have been wounded, was to meet them, so he arranged for us to visit the Walter Reed National Military Medical Center in Bethesda, Maryland. It was a trip as affecting as the day I walked around West Point. We encountered soldiers, sailors, and Marines who had lost arms and legs, and suffered severe brain trauma and burns, from improvised explosive devices. These young people had been dealt the worst hand life can offer. Despite astounding advances in prosthetics, many face a lifetime of pain and physical restriction, of arduous rehabilitation and lengthy hospitalizations. Yet through it all, they are among the most optimistic people I've ever met. They want to heal, and they slog through daily physical therapy sessions, learning how to walk on artificial legs, struggling to write their names and button their shirts, because they want to rejoin their buddies and continue serving.

Some of them do. Others go on to perform even more amazing feats. Over lunch in the cafeteria, I sat next to Cedric King, an Army sergeant first class who lost both of his legs to a land mine in Afghanistan in 2012. He spoke of his injury, of regaining consciousness eight days later at an Army hospital in Germany, surrounded by his family. As he reflected on his life, he dwelled on the eight years he spent in the military, his combat deployments, and the bonds he forged with his fellow soldiers. "I wouldn't change a thing," he said. At that moment, I felt as small as the saltshaker on the table. King spoke excitedly about his recovery and said he was training to run the 2014 Boston Marathon. Two months after our meeting, he crossed the finish line.

As we wrapped up the visit that afternoon, I had resolved to myself that I couldn't be a bystander when it came to our veterans; I couldn't simply say "thank you" and move on. I had met extraordinary people. I had to do something.

Through my encounters with our active-duty troops and veterans—and their former leaders—it became clear to me that the Americans who have participated in the Iraq and Afghanistan wars face a dual challenge: tens of thousands have grave injuries that will require an enormous ongoing financial commitment—for their medical care, for the well-being of their families, for research into new treatments for their ailments—but those who are healthy and eager to join the workforce are too often viewed as damaged goods by a nation that has become disconnected from those who have served.

To assist with the financial need, Sheri and I have pledged to spend significant funds through our family foundation on programs to help veterans navigate the challenges of returning to civilian life. To address the civilian-military disconnect, I decided to team up with Rajiv Chandrasekaran, a *Washington Post* journalist who has spent years in Iraq and Afghanistan writing about our troops.

RAJIV'S REFLECTIONS

After so much time in war zones, I thought there wasn't much I could find shocking anymore. Certainly not a spreadsheet.

A few weeks before Howard visited Walter Reed, I sat in my office poring over pages of data from an unprecedented poll of

Iraq and Afghanistan veterans conducted by the *Post* and the Kaiser Family Foundation. In the tallies of responses to seventy-eight questions, recorded as letters and numbers printed in black ink, a stunning portrait of our modern warriors emerged. I blinked, wondering if I was reading the findings incorrectly.

Of the 2.6 million Americans dispatched to fight, more than half said their mental or physical health is worse than before they deployed, and 18 percent—about 470,000 current and former service members—reported being seriously injured while deployed to Iraq or Afghanistan, or in support of the conflicts. One in two said they know a fellow service member who has attempted or committed suicide, and more than 1 million reported suffering from relationship problems and outbursts of anger.

They were deeply disappointed by the assistance provided by the Pentagon and the Department of Veterans Affairs. One and a half million of those who served in the wars said the needs of their fellow vets are not being met by the government. Even so, the vast majority of recent veterans are not embittered or regretful. Considering everything they now know about war and military service, almost 90 percent said they would still have joined.

But what really stunned me was a question we posed about the nation they so faithfully served: 55 percent—about 1.4 million veterans among this generation—said they feel disconnected from civilian life in America. When I shared the data with Howard, that response, more than any other, drew a gasp. How could the America outside military bases feel so alien to our veterans? It revealed a giant divide between our military and our civilian populations.

When Howard proposed collaborating on a book about veterans, I agreed without hesitation. Although I was far more familiar with the military—I had traveled extensively with our troops in Iraq and Afghanistan, walking foot patrols, surviving firefights, befriending warriors across ranks and services—I hadn't begun to understand their experience as veterans until working on the *Post* poll. In the first few months of 2014, I crisscrossed the country to speak at length with dozens of men and women who had participated in the wars. I returned to my home in our nation's capital convinced that their stories had to be shared with my fellow Americans.

OUR BOOK

We thank them for their service. We applaud them at sporting events. But how much do we really know about who our veterans are, what they did overseas, what they're doing now? In many homes, unlike in previous generations, these stories aren't shared across the dinner table. Less than 1 percent of our population have served our military abroad since the September 11, 2001, attacks. Add their direct family members, and they still amount to less than 5 percent of the nation. Most Americans have no skin in the game.

A major reason is the way our countrymen have come to wear the uniform. With no draft, we rely on brave volunteers. It is a system that has provided us with the best-trained, most-disciplined military in the world, and even during the most difficult periods of the Iraq war, there was never a shortage of young men and women who were willing to join. The reliance on volunteers has led many other Americans to pay scant attention to the sacrifice of our warriors. We let them protect us, yet we go on with life as usual. Political leaders have encouraged us to do so, as have the media. Television networks for the most part turned their attention elsewhere after the opening months of both wars.

Most of these veterans are now home, so why bother? In fact, our engagement is more important than ever. They don't need care packages and quilts. They need a nation to understand the skills and values and discipline they have acquired—and the assistance they still require—and then give them an opportunity to make a difference on the home front. They need to return to a nation that feels connected to them.

We believe we speak for most Americans in saying we want this generation of veterans to be welcomed in the same way our country embraced their brethren who fought in World War II, not in the sometimes-shameful manner that those who served in Vietnam were regarded. The Greatest Generation could take comfort in the knowledge that they had achieved a clear-cut victory. The wars in Iraq and Afghanistan will have an unsatisfactory outcome in the eyes of many, including many who fought there, and that only exacerbates the challenge some veterans will face as they seek to make sense of their years in combat. Regardless of whether you think the wars were worthy missions or fool's errands, we must remember that those who deployed were not the ones who decided to launch the invasions, the surges, the pullouts. They followed orders from civilian leaders of both parties, nobly and unflinchingly.

We hope this book will motivate Americans on both sides—our veterans and active-duty service members, and those who haven't served and don't possess a direct family tie to a veteran—to collaborate in communities across our country to close this gap. Saying "thank you" at an airport is not enough. Standing for an ovation at a baseball game is not enough. To do right by our veterans—to recognize their value to our society and fulfill our solemn obligation to those who volunteered to protect the rest of us—we first have to understand what they have accomplished and what they offer our nation.

The first half of this book describes acts of remarkable valor by service members in Iraq and Afghanistan, among them an Army sergeant who repeatedly ran into a hail of gunfire to protect his comrades, two Marines who chose to stand and defend their outpost and thirty-three comrades from an oncoming truck bomb instead of running to safety, and a sixty-year-old doctor who joined the Navy and saved the lives of dozens after his son was killed at war.

The second half shows how post-9/11 veterans are plowing their leadership skills and commitment to service into initiatives to strengthen and improve our nation. Among them are former soldiers who help residents dig out after natural disasters, those who are turning around inner-city neighborhoods, a general seeking new ways to treat brain trauma, and a group of spouses who assist severely wounded warriors. You will see the challenges some of our returning troops face—unemployment, homelessness, post-traumatic stress—but you will also learn of the remarkable skills they have acquired and the courage they continue to display.

We conclude with a discussion of ways we can work together to bridge the gap in our society between civilians and service members.

We hope you will find these stories humbling and inspiring, revealing and engaging. In this era of ideological bickering and incessant self-absorption, our nation has no shortage of men and women of uncommon valor.

Part One

CHAPTER ONE

In His Son's Steps

As soon as Bill Krissoff glanced out the front window during breakfast to see who had rung his doorbell at eight on a Saturday morning, he knew. Three Marines, ramrod straight in their dress blues, stood next to an Army chaplain.

Nate, Krissoff's elder son, twenty-five years old, had deployed to Iraq with an elite reconnaissance battalion as a first lieutenant in the Marine Corps.

"We regret to inform you," one of the Marines began saying once Krissoff opened the door. He doesn't remember the rest. His head spinning, his body seized with shock, he stumbled through the house to wake up Christine, his wife. Soon they were sitting together on a living room sofa as the Marines explained, with grim solemnity, what had occurred a half day earlier half a world away from their home in Reno, Nevada.

Nathan M. Krissoff, a counterintelligence specialist, had been returning to his base from a village near Fallujah when his Humvee drove over a bomb buried in a dry riverbed. The brunt of the blast hit the vehicle's right side. Nate had been in the right rear seat.

The Marines sat stoically, awaiting the next question Bill or Christine would ask.

The Krissoffs wanted to call their other son, Austin, at the Marine Corps' Officer Candidates School in Quantico, Virginia.

Less than three years younger than Nate, he was following his brother's trail from an elite prep school in Pebble Beach, California, to a small New England liberal arts college, and then into military service.

The Krissoffs aren't one of those families in which every male for the last four generations has worn a uniform. Bill, who came of age during the Vietnam War, wasn't drafted and didn't volunteer. Nate hadn't been on the military track. In high school, he wrote poetry, played in the school symphony, and enjoyed wild-water kayaking. At Williams College in Massachusetts, which doesn't have an Army or Marine ROTC program, he captained the swim team and majored in political science.

Then came September 11, 2001. He was a junior. The father of his best friend on the swim team, a New York banker, did nothing for six weeks but go to funerals. Nate's carefree ways began to turn more serious. A year after he graduated, he applied for a job with the CIA. At his interview, the recruiter was impressed with Nate's education and aptitude but urged him to get some seasoning before pursuing such a career. Crestfallen, Nate contacted a friend from Williams who had become a Marine intelligence officer. If he wanted seasoning, his friend said, the Marines would give it to him.

In June 2004, as the Iraq war was becoming ever more perilous for American troops, Nate told his father that he wanted to become a Marine officer. Bill was more than a little apprehensive.

"Do you fully understand what this means?" he asked his son. "Do you understand the risk?"

Nate said he did.

Three months later, Nate was marching across the parade field at Quantico, a newly commissioned second lieutenant. Bill and Christine sat in the bleachers, as proud as the other parents, but understandably anxious. *This is the real deal,* Bill thought to himself as he watched his lanky son in the distance, standing at attention, his thick, dark hair shorn into a Marine-regulation high-and-tight buzz cut under his cap.

But before Nate could be called into a battle zone, there would be Basic School, where he was taught the art and science of leading Marines. Then intelligence school. Then an assignment on Okinawa. It was there that he talked his way into an Iraq deployment with the Third Reconnaissance Battalion.

As he headed to Iraq in September 2006, he sent an e-mail to his parents and Austin, who had graduated from college and was preparing to enter Marine officer school.

> Almost five years to the day after September 11, 2001, I have the chance to put my money where my mouth is in terms of service . . . I'm constantly reminded of that famous quote from Tom Hanks' character at the end of *Saving Private Ryan:* "Earn this." Earning it will mean sacrifice, determination, doing my job to the best of my ability. I chose this, and I wouldn't have it any other way.
>
> The complexities of the conflict and the shifting perceptions of the world are all but totally irrelevant to the fact that we fight for the men at our side; my success will be gauged by the responsibility to safeguard Marines and accomplish the mission, not by any other metric. I'm lucky to be deploying with such a phenomenal, savvy group of guys.

Several weeks later, Nate wrote to Austin, who had started school at Quantico, with a description of an attack that killed Sergeant Jonathan J. Simpson, a much-admired member of the recon battalion.

Why do I tell you this? Because Sgt. Simpson and many all-Americans like him are the ones you will be entrusted to lead, protect and stand in front of. Never forget that all the trials and training you and the other candidates (eventually Second Lieutenants) go through is not about you. America's sons and daughters will be entrusted to your care. You owe them competence, discipline, courage, judgment, etc. Post Sgt. Simpson's memorial picture, perhaps up on your squad bay read-board, tell your fire team and squad and platoon about him—as a clear reminder of what this is all about. Keep it with you through the trials ahead. Because when you hear the final roll call, the long bugle playing taps, and the bagpipes wailing—we better have done everything short of the hand of God Himself to accomplish the mission and bring Marines home. It is a sacrifice he and many like him have made fighting for each other. Earn it.

When Nate became the 2,924th American service member killed in Operation Iraqi Freedom on December 9, 2006, Austin was almost finished with officer school. He wanted to stay with his training platoon, "the only people," he thought, "who understood what happened." But the staff at Quantico put him on a flight to Reno.

His mother hoped he would reconsider his decision to be a Marine—the service offered him the choice of walking away because he was his parents' only surviving child—but he would not change his mind. Nate "would have wanted nothing more than for me to carry on the mission," he said. But to partly assuage his mother's concerns, he decided that instead of going into the infantry as he had planned, he would specialize in intelligence, as his brother had, though in a noncombat role. A week after he arrived in Reno, he was commissioned as an officer in a low-key swearing-in at his parents' house.

On the Saturday before Christmas, the Krissoffs held a memorial service for Nate in Reno. White-gloved Marines hoisted a flag-draped coffin containing an urn with Nate's cremated ashes. The national anthem was played. A teacher at Nate's high school recalled his warmth, his love of literature, and his mischievous side. "As a young man Nate was, indeed, Dickens' Pip, Salinger's Holden, and Twain's Huck. But he was also Ferris Bueller." A friend from Williams described him as "goofy, hilarious, and charismatic on the outside but disciplined, insightful, and focused on the inside." Captain Michael Dubrule, who had led Nate through intelligence training, told the mourners that Nate skillfully collected information to help save the lives of American troops and innocent Iraqis. "I want you all to know that Nate died doing what he loved, leading men in combat, saving lives, and making a difference in the lives of so many," Dubrule said. "No greater epitaph can be written, no greater sacrifice can be made."

After a few weeks, Bill threw himself back into his work as an orthopedic surgeon. Chris joined him in the office, where she ran the business side of his solo practice. He returned to the operating theater. Grief welled inside him, but his skill as a physician was undiminished. Soon, however, treating busted shoulders and bum knees—as he had for twenty-eight years—began to feel unfulfilling. One day that spring, a patient came in complaining of minor knee pain, the sort of ache that would go away with some rest or a varied workout routine.

Why, Bill thought, *am I spending my time hearing people complain about nothing?*

A few months later, Nate's battalion commander, Lieutenant Colonel William Seely, traveling the country to visit the parents of his fallen Marines, came to see the Krissoff family. Bill and Austin took him for a hike around Lake Tahoe's Emerald Bay, and Bill asked Seely about medical care for Marines in Iraq. Seely told him that every Marine battalion deploys with a surgeon and numerous medics, all from the Navy. As Seely described the role of the battalion surgeon, the penny dropped for Bill.

That's what I want to do, he thought. *I want to be a battalion surgeon.*

Bill was as lean as his boys. He stayed fit by biking, hiking, kayaking, and skiing. He figured he could meet the military's physical requirements, so he called up a Navy recruiter in San Francisco and offered up his services. The recruiter posed a series of questions. Finally, he asked how old Bill was.

"Sixty," Bill said.

"Um, that's a problem," the recruiter replied. "You're too old."

Anyone over forty-two who wants to join the Navy Reserve medical corps needs an age waiver, the recruiter explained. He wasn't optimistic about the possibility of a sixty-year-old obtaining one.

Undeterred, Krissoff called an Air Force recruiter. He got a similar answer. So he went back to treating sore knees.

That August, he and Christine received a voice-mail message from a White House aide inviting them to meet with President George W. Bush after he spoke to an American Legion convention in Reno the following week. They attended the speech with Austin, standing in the back and laughing at the president's self-deprecating humor. As the president was concluding his remarks, they were ushered into a small room with several other families. All of them were "gold star" parents and siblings, those who had lost sons or daughters, brothers or sisters, in Iraq or Afghanistan.

Bush strode in a few minutes later and shook everyone's hand. He spoke at length about the war, explaining his strategy and lauding the sacrifice of his audience's fallen relatives. The Krissoffs listened intently. Iraq was being torn apart by a civil war. U.S. troops were getting attacked daily. Hundreds of Americans had come back in caskets since Nate's final journey home. The war had become deeply unpopular: fewer than four in ten Americans still believed it was worth fighting. When Bush asked for questions or comments, Bill spoke up. He knew what had driven Nate to join the Marines, to find his way to Iraq. He didn't want his son to have died in vain.

"Let's stay the course," he told the president.

Bush approached each family individually and asked if there was anything he could do to help them. Several made small requests for assistance in dealing with death-benefits paperwork. An aide dutifully jotted notes.

Then Bush walked over to the Krissoffs and posed the same question.

"Yes, sir. There is one thing," Bill said. "I want to join the Navy medical corps and serve, but they told me I was too old. No disrespect, but I'm younger than you are."

Bush's eyes widened. He looked at Christine.

"What does Mom think?"

Christine said she and Bill had talked about his desire to serve. She wasn't thrilled with the prospect of his traveling to a war zone, but she wouldn't stand in the way if going might help her husband heal. "I'm on board with it," she said.

Bush turned to Austin, who had driven up from Camp Pendleton to accompany his parents to the meeting. He was skeptical, but he, too, didn't want to sabotage his father's quest. "He'll be pretty good out there," he told the president.

Bush said he would be meeting with General Peter Pace, the chairman of the Joint Chiefs of Staff, in two days and would mention Krissoff's request. He summoned Karl Rove, one of his top aides, to collect the necessary information from Bill.

"I'll see what I can do," Bush said.

Three days after meeting Bush, Krissoff received a phone call from the same Navy recruiter who had scoffed at his request to join a few months earlier. "I have orders to meet with you by the end of the day," the recruiter said. When Krissoff replied that he was trailering a horse with his wife and could not immediately drive down to San Francisco—three hours away by car—the recruiter was undeterred. "I'm coming up to see you," he said.

Krissoff took the recruiter to dinner, filled out a stack of paperwork—and waited. A month later, he got word that he had been accepted into the Navy Reserve for his dream assignment: a Marine Corps medical battalion.

Although he was required to train once a month, Krissoff treated his reserve duties as a full-time job. For him, joining the military wasn't about wearing a uniform and attending to Marines on the home front. He wanted to go to Iraq, as Nate had done and Austin would be doing soon. And that meant spending as much time as possible learning how to be a combat physician. He had decades of medical experience, but none of that involved treating blast wounds.

He and his wife moved to the San Diego area in early 2008 so he could be closer to the Navy hospital on the Marine Corps air base in Miramar, where he signed up for every combat-medicine course he could take. He traveled to Morocco that summer to participate in a military exercise during which he practiced working in a field hospital. He attended advanced workshops at an Army hospital in Texas, and he joined Marines on heart-thumping hikes through the rocky Southern California hills to prove to superiors a generation younger that he could withstand the rigors of deployment.

When his training felt grueling, he thought back to a letter Nate had written while he was at officer school:

o dark 30. 4:30 a.m. Then it began. Platoon staff formally introduced us and then took charge. Imagine tables flipping, chairs getting thrown against walls, instructors screaming. A volume that shocks the body. PT has been harder than any work I've done in my life . . . Pain is constant here. Honor, sacrifice, integrity aren't just fairytale phrases. They're earned every day in sweat, tears, blood, etc., by these people. The values of the USMC are one of a kind. Keep shit straight . . . The more you sweat in peace, the less you bleed in war.

Austin, who was stationed at Pendleton at the time, came by to watch his father put on his uniform. "He'd shake his head and redo everything," Bill said with a chuckle.

BILL KRISSOFF AND HIS SON NATE

Eighteen months after meeting President Bush, in February 2009, Bill Krissoff arrived in Iraq—as a lieutenant commander in the Navy—to spend seven months treating orthopedic injuries at a field hospital on the sprawling al-Taqaddum Air Base near Fallujah, less than ten miles from where Nate had been killed.

For Bill, the decision to go to war at sixty-two had nothing to do with seeking closure after his son's death. The term itself provoked him. " 'Closure' is for somebody else," he said. "That's not for people who have lost sons and daughters. Your life has changed. Forever changed . . . You don't just have closure and move on with your life."

Shuttering his lucrative medical practice, joining the Navy, and deploying to the western Iraqi desert was about "turning that loss into something positive." Nate's commitment to service—to his nation, to his fellow Marines—and Austin's decision to follow in his brother's path had not just filled Bill with pride. Their devotion had humbled him. As he took stock of his life in the bleak months after losing Nate, he concluded that he needed to be more like his boys. He possessed skills that could help save lives and limbs in a land of IEDs. He needed to put himself to better use, even if it meant leaving his luxurious home, his comfortable job, his devoted wife.

"In most cases, fathers inspire sons," he said. "In this case, sons inspire Dad."

By the time Bill reached Iraq, the war was winding down. Sunni Muslim tribesmen in Fallujah, Ramadi, and across the western desert, once mortal enemies of the United States, were now collaborating with the Marines to beat back al-Qaeda militants. The hospital at al-Taqaddum, which had been among the busiest trauma centers in the country just two years earlier, could go a full week without a serious casualty. Bill found himself treating sore knees and shoulders, just as he had back home, and teaching young corpsmen how to attend to orthopedic wounds. He had time to visit Austin, who was stationed at another large Marine base in western Iraq.

When Bill returned home that fall, his wife and son assumed his thirst for deployment had been satiated. They knew he wouldn't be going back to his Reno practice, but they expected him to transition to full-time work at the Pendleton hospital, which he did—for a few weeks. Then he got word that a position was open on the next rotation of doctors to Afghanistan. The captain in charge, one of the pioneers of combat surgery, wanted Krissoff to join him. Bill hadn't even unpacked his bags from Iraq.

"I know I've been gone, but this is probably an opportunity that won't come up again," he told Christine. "I'm not getting any younger. And I'm all trained up."

She looked him in the eyes. "Well," she said, "you better go."

Krissoff began work at the main trauma center at Camp Bastion, in southwestern Afghanistan, in February 2010, the same month Marines commenced a bloody assault on Marjah, a Taliban sanctuary riddled with snipers and makeshift antipersonnel mines. His first case was a triple amputee. Over the next seven months, he would serve as the primary or assisting surgeon on 225 serious casualties. He lost count of the number of amputations he performed.

He had expected a caseload unlike anything he had experienced in the civilian world—before joining the military, he had performed only one multiple amputation in his career, on a drunk who had fallen onto a train track—but nothing could have prepared him for the frequency of horrific injuries that rolled through the trauma bay doors at the hospital at Camp Bastion. There were times when all five operating tables were in use, and Krissoff had to scurry among them. He and his fellow doctors once performed twenty-four surgeries in a single day. "All you're thinking about is how to patch them up," he said. "You're cranking."

Back then, Afghanistan was an orthopedic surgeon's war. In the southern deserts that were the focus of President Obama's troop surge, the Taliban's weapon of choice was a five-liter plastic jug packed with homemade, fertilizer-based explosives, buried in the ground and triggered with a balsa-wood pressure plate. It was crude but ingenious: because the only metal parts in the device were tiny pieces of wire, it was nearly invisible to American bomb detectors. If a U.S. or Afghan trooper stepped on one, the force of the explosion was usually enough to sever a leg or two, and perhaps an arm.

A generation ago, such wounds were often fatal. By 2010, however, all U.S. service members in that part of Afghanistan kept two or more tourniquets affixed to their ballistic vests, allowing comrades to stanch the bleeding from severed limbs. Medical evacuation helicopters would bring the wounded to Camp Bastion in less than an hour. Then the really difficult work would begin: agonizing about where to amputate; cauterizing blood vessels; searching for shrapnel inside the abdomen; combating infections; trying to ensure young men would be capable of fathering a child when they healed. If a patient arrived at the Camp Bastion hospital with a heartbeat, he or she had a 97 percent chance of surviving.

When he wasn't working shifts that could stretch to sixteen hours, depending on the pace of medevac choppers alighting at the hospital's landing pad, Krissoff slept in a tent he shared with ten other medical personnel. He didn't have more than a few days off in seven months.

"There wasn't any 'No, I'm not doing that today. I'm off.' Everybody just works when you need help."

Despite the intensity and privation, the daily exposure to the horrors of war, those seven months were the most rewarding time in Krissoff's three-decade-long orthopedic career. It wasn't the challenge or the adventure. It was about the Marines and others in his care. He chatted up those who could talk, reveling in their stories.

He treated one sergeant who had been shot in the arm in Marjah and was missing a chunk of his bicep. "Doc," the Marine told him, "you need to know one thing: I returned fire." Krissoff cleaned out the bullet hole—it was the simplest case he had treated in weeks—and told the Marine he'd be sent home. "What do you mean 'home'?" the Marine said. "I'm going back to my unit."

To minimize the chance of infection, military doctors prefer to leave many wounds open for several days, with just a gauze cover, as opposed to stitching them up right away. Krissoff struck a deal with the Marine: once he closed the wound, the Marine could return to Marjah.

A few weeks later, Krissoff treated another Marine from the same unit. "How's that sergeant doing?" he asked.

"He got shot again—this time, in the hip," the other Marine said. "But he got treated in Kandahar, and he's back on duty again."

Where do we get these guys? Krissoff thought. *He's a war fighter. He's not going to give up. He's not going home. His guys are still there. You can't explain that to most civilians.*

Marines who learned Krissoff's story would come up to thank him in the dining hall. He'd always turn it around. "Thank you for what *you* are doing," he'd often say. "*Your* service humbles me."

Military doctors in field hospitals are loath to take sole credit for treating patients. "It's a team effort. You don't do this stuff by yourself," Krissoff said. But senior officers familiar with his work readily volunteer what he is too modest to divulge: he led or assisted surgical teams that saved dozens of American, British, and Afghan lives.

"He made an enormous contribution," said Stephen F. McCartney, a now-retired Navy captain who served as the command surgeon to the Marine brigade in southwestern Afghanistan when Krissoff began his deployment. McCartney said Krissoff's age was an invaluable asset. "He brought experience and judgment that can only come with many years of practicing medicine," McCartney said.

Major General Larry Nicholson, who had been Nate's regimental commander in Iraq, served as the top Marine general in southern Afghanistan for the initial months of Krissoff's time at the Camp Bastion hospital. "Bill made a difference for good every day," said Nicholson. "There can be no greater act of love by a father for his fallen son than to take his place in the ranks in the midst of war."

For James Raffetto, as for so many of those who wound up on Krissoff's operating table, it was horrible luck that got him there. A single footfall on a bit of earth in southern Afghanistan that was home to a bomb.

Raffetto was a strapping, Pennsylvania-raised Navy medic. Not a medical doctor like Krissoff, but a corpsman. He traveled with elite reconnaissance Marines in the field—as Nate had—treating wounds until the medevac birds arrived. His platoon had been patrolling a small desert village used by the Taliban as a staging area for attacks on Marine units based in nearby farming communities. It had been an easy day. The houses suspected to be insurgent hideouts were empty, and residents had been willing to talk to the Marines. (Taliban intimidation usually tied their tongues.) One father even asked Raffetto to examine his sick daughter.

As they departed from the last insurgent compound, Raffetto spotted a box of gauze on the ground. *Ah, this must be a Taliban field hospital,* he thought. He took a step toward the box, and the ground rose with an earsplitting boom. He flew into the air. A second later, he slammed into the ground facedown. He tried to turn over, but he couldn't. As he winced in pain, a platoon mate flipped him on his back. Raffetto opened his eyes and looked down.

Left leg gone.

Right leg gone.

Left arm dangling by a tendon.

Right arm intact, but battered and bleeding.

"Doc," one of the Marines called out, "tell us what to do."

Raffetto knew that if he was to survive, he needed to cut off the blood gushing from his limbs. With his right hand, he grabbed a tourniquet off his ballistic vest and wrapped it around his left arm above the elbow. Then he directed his comrades to do the same for his legs, and to shoot him up with morphine.

They strapped a standard-issue nylon and plastic tourniquet on his left thigh. Then they tried to do the same on his right side. But so much of his leg was gone that they needed to cinch the band near his hip, at the widest part of his meaty thigh. The tourniquet broke. As did a second one. As death from blood loss grew imminent, a quick-thinking sergeant took off his canvas belt and pulled it around Raffetto's thigh. Then he grabbed a spare machine gun barrel, pushed it between the belt and the leg, and twisted it around to tighten the belt and cut off the flow of blood.

Through it all, Raffetto remained conscious.

I'm fucked up, he thought, *but I don't think I'm gonna die.*

As they waited for the medevac chopper, he joked with his buddies, who knelt around him. "Survive!" he said to them—and himself—doing his best to imitate Sergeant Lincoln Osiris in the movie farce *Tropic Thunder.* And he asked them to give a message to his wife. "Tell Emily I love her."

A British evacuation helicopter arrived in less than fifteen minutes. As Raffetto was hoisted aboard, the flight nurse asked him how he felt.

What a charming accent, he thought. Then he passed out.

When Raffetto arrived at the Camp Bastion hospital, Krissoff didn't know where to begin. He had seen terrible trauma, but nothing like this. His patient was a pile of bloodied flesh atop a gurney.

"This guy is in bad shape," he muttered to himself. Treating such grievous wounds sometimes prompted a quiet doubt. *What are we doing? Are we saving people who are going to have no life?* But he pushed the thought out of his head. Here was a fellow American. A sailor. A young man who had volunteered to serve his nation. Krissoff vowed to do all he could to save the patient.

He and his fellow physicians sealed off blood vessels. They cleaned the exposed tissue. They sought to salvage as much of Raffetto's right hand as possible.

A day later, Raffetto was bundled on a C-17 transport aircraft and flown to the Army's hospital in Landstuhl, Germany, and then on to the Navy's medical center in Bethesda. Unlike Krissoff's patients in the civilian world, whom he would check up on in the days after surgery, he knew he would not see Raffetto again. That was true of most of his patients. Did they bounce back quickly? Suffer more complications? Succumb to the injuries? He usually had no idea.

A little more than a year later, after Krissoff had returned to his home in Rancho Santa Fe, California, he tracked down Raffetto's phone number. When he called, Raffetto's wife, Emily, picked up. They had been married for just four months before James deployed. But she never wavered when he returned to America covered in bandages, connected to half a dozen tubes, and missing three limbs. She remained by his side as he convalesced in Bethesda for two years, first as an inpatient and later as a daily member of the rehabilitation center, where he was fitted with prosthetics and slowly, painfully learned to walk again.

Krissoff asked Emily if he could talk to his former patient.

"I'm sure he'd like to," she replied. "But we're on our way to renew our vows."

Later that afternoon, clad in his Navy dress uniform, Raffetto walked down the aisle with his bride.

Eventually, doctor and patient did connect. When they did, Raffetto told Krissoff that he was learning to drive a handicap-enabled truck and looking for work.

"You're just amazing," Krissoff told him.

"Thanks to you," Raffetto replied.

Krissoff began calling periodically. It wasn't medical curiosity that drove him to keep in touch. He admired the young man's perseverance, his don't-dwell-on-the-negative attitude. As Raffetto shared milestones in his recovery—landing a full-time job with the federal government, fending for himself for three weeks while Emily was on a trip to Europe—Krissoff's cheers were valuable reminders to Raffetto that he wasn't just healing, he was thriving.

As amazed as Krissoff was at Raffetto's recovery, Raffetto was similarly awed as he came to learn Bill's story through their calls.

"To join the military at sixty—wow," Raffetto said as he zipped through his kitchen in a power-assisted wheelchair. "And not like he tried, someone said no, and he said, 'Well, all right.'"

Raffetto pulled up to his dining table and thought for a moment.

"You can be a war hero even if you never fired a weapon in combat," he said. "What he did—now, that's uncommon valor."

CHAPTER TWO

Never Leave a Fallen Comrade

Swoop in by helicopter under the cover of darkness. Surround the walled-off desert redoubt of a Taliban subcommander planning a wave of suicide bombings in the city of Kandahar. Capture him and his two confederates if possible, or kill them all if they put up a fight. A few more bad guys taken out of circulation, a few more innocent Afghans saved.

The mission would require only fifteen minutes on the ground, maybe thirty, leaving enough time for the elite Army Rangers to fly back to their base and hit the gym before bedtime.

It was early in the evening of October 5, 2013. A high-flying drone had been circling the Taliban compound all day. Nothing in the video footage raised flags among those in the operations center planning the raid. As the members of the Ranger assault team were briefed on the mission, similar thoughts went through their heads: *Routine. Benign. Low risk.*

They would be cops executing an arrest warrant—Afghan-style. The intention was to avoid firing a round. The Rangers would bring along a team of Afghan army commandos, who would order the insurgents outside, then search, handcuff, and blindfold them.

To approach a target undetected, Rangers are often dropped off a few miles away and skulk toward their prey, each with as much as one hundred pounds of gear. But for this operation, a dual-rotor

Chinook would deposit them just a short jog from the compound of the subcommander, code-named Ares 102.

This is going to be fun, thought Sergeant Tom Block, a linebacker-sized team leader who had turned twenty-seven the day before. An easy night, as the assault on the Ares 102 compound appeared to promise, was rare. Block's unit, the First Platoon of Bravo Company of the Third Battalion of the Seventy-Fifth Ranger Regiment, had been working at a hectic pace during the six weeks they had been in Afghanistan. By that point in the Afghan war, some Army units were spending more time on base than off. When they did venture out, it was almost always to support Afghan forces, who were supposed to be leading the fight against the Taliban. But life was different for the Rangers. Their job wasn't to babysit Afghan troops but to hunt senior and mid-level Taliban leaders—the men responsible for organizing, funding, and equipping the insurgency. Ranger battalions, which fall under the military's secretive Joint Special Operations Command while deployed to war zones, had been conducting these missions in Afghanistan continuously since October 2001. Although the Rangers, including several members of First Platoon, had been instrumental in beating the Taliban back across the southern part of the country, the insurgents were far from spent. New leaders, armed with money and munitions, kept streaming over the border from Pakistan. That meant new targets for First Platoon and the rest of Third Battalion.

Kelan Horton, a staff sergeant who led one of the four squads that made up First Platoon, had awakened just before sunset. His first order of business was to go to the platoon's tactical operations center—the TOC—a locked room with top secret computer terminals and video monitors displaying live feeds from drones flying over their area of responsibility. There he learned about the plan to capture Ares 102. An intelligence report had arrived that day with the Taliban subcommander's location. Concerned that he would

MEMBERS OF FIRST PLATOON, BRAVO COMPANY, THIRD BATTALION,
SEVENTY-FIFTH RANGER REGIMENT

soon move elsewhere, U.S. commanders had put him atop their list
of targets. He would be pursued that night, if weather permitted
and no more pressing crises emerged.

While Horton was in the TOC with other leaders, junior members of the platoon rolled out of bed at the normal dinner hour
and hit the gym. Because they prefer to strike their targets in the
dark, Rangers at war are a nocturnal bunch. Although raid nights
mean no long, depleting runs beforehand, lifting weights is part of
their daily routine, as ingrained as brushing their teeth. The junior
members soon joined Horton and other leaders in a briefing room,
where Captain Peter Leszczynski, Bravo Company's commander,
told them about the mission to nab Ares 102. Leszczynski assigned
the raid to First Platoon. His Second Platoon would remain on
standby on the vast NATO air base south of Kandahar city, serving as a quick-reaction force if needed. He said First Platoon's four

squads, each comprising eight men, would be split up: two of them would deal with Ares 102; the other two would head to another target, a village two miles away, separated by a line of steep hills, where more than a dozen of Ares 102's foot soldiers were believed to be hiding.

The two squads going after Ares 102 would be divided further. One would team up with the Afghan commandos to surround the compound. The other would pursue the third person on the site, who was loitering outside the compound as a lookout. Because Leszczynski expected the loiterer to try to run away as soon as the Rangers arrived, he called him "the squirter." He told his soldiers to be vigilant, but he wasn't expecting much resistance. He thought the chance of getting into a gunfight was less than 1 percent.

As the electronic thump of Lady Gaga's song "Poker Face" filled their plywood-walled ready room, First Platoon suited up: flak vests, night-vision goggles, radio headsets under their Kevlar helmets, clips of 5.56-millimeter ammunition for their M4 carbines, more ammo clips, grenades, first-aid kits. Most Rangers also carried an American flag, either wrapped around the ballistic plates in their vests or rolled up in pouches affixed to their belts.

The members of First Platoon hustled onto the tarmac and boarded two Special Operations MH-47 Chinooks. The black-painted helicopters, piloted by some of the Army's most skilled aviators, lifted off at midnight. Fifteen minutes later, one of the choppers set down near the target site. The assault force—twenty-eight American military personnel, four Afghan commandos, one interpreter, and one military dog—began filing out the rear ramp at a run.

One squad was supposed to head to the compound, but the chopper's rotors had whipped up a dust cloud so thick that the Rangers couldn't see the infrared light beamed on the target through their night-vision scopes. Two members of the squad assigned to the compound walked past it. So, too, did the Afghan soldiers.

The six who headed the right way made it to the compound in two minutes. The mud-walled structure was half-built and empty. Next to it, inside a courtyard surrounded by a flimsy, chest-high fabric fence, were a makeshift tent and a tarp on which were arranged boxes and bags. Amid this clutter, a man sat serenely alongside a figure dressed head to toe in a burka.

The Rangers fanned out along two sides of the fence. Generally, if the Rangers were detected as they approached a house, their targets cowered, put up a fight, or fled. These two just sat there.

This is shady, thought Horton.

"They looked guilty," Tom Block recalled. "Really guilty."

Horton told Block, who was closest to the only opening in the fence, and other Rangers nearby to hold their positions until the Afghan commandos arrived.

With the Rangers' interpreter also missing, Block tried to recall a few rudimentary phrases in Pashto, the local language. He ordered the man to stand and lift up his tunic. When the man did so, Block gave a brief sigh of relief. He wasn't rigged with a bomb.

Sit back down, Block instructed, and put your hands up.

The man complied—for a moment. Then he got up and began walking toward Block.

Wadrega! Block shouted. Stop!

But the man kept coming, trailed by the figure in the burka. When the man was two feet away, Block grabbed his shirt collar and spun him around.

The burka-clad figure drew nearer.

Wadrega!

The person under the fabric seemed to have remarkably broad shoulders for a woman, and an unusually long gait.

That's a dude, Block thought.

At that instant, whoever was under the burka leaped toward Block. Before he could raise his M4 or shout again, night switched to day, the crisp air turned infernal, and the burka blasted apart in a cloud of blood and bone. Block heard the ear-shattering blast as he hurtled backward.

He landed on his back in a ditch. He had seen a brilliant white light, then blackness. *Am I dead?* he wondered. Then he heard a second explosion. He'd learn later that the insurgents had rigged their tent to blow seconds after the suicide bomb detonated.

I guess I'm still here.

Block wiggled his fingers. He wiggled his toes.

Got 'em.

He was damned lucky to be alive. The man he had grabbed had shielded him from the worst of the blast.

Block tried to look around, but he couldn't see a thing. He chalked it up to losing his night-vision goggles. He remained silent.

As he was told in Ranger school, if there's a follow-on ambush, you'll give away your position to the attackers if you shout out. But after a minute, he concluded there was no second-wave assault.

"Help! Over here," he called out. "Help! Over here."

As he waited for someone to arrive, he thought about his fiancée, Janine. *This is the end of Rangering. She'll never let me deploy again.*

Then he raised his middle finger in the direction of the explosion.

You ain't getting me today.

Michael Remley, a staff sergeant who had joined the mission that night as a second medic—assault teams normally have one—ran up to Block.

"Oh, my God," Remley gasped.

"Thanks, Doc," Block grunted.

Remley went to work on Block, slapping tourniquets on his thighs and inserting three needles into his chest to normalize pressure around his heart. Block told him his face hurt the worst. Parts of it had been burned off, and though Block didn't realize it yet, his right eye was missing. Remley jammed gauze in the socket.

As Remley worked on Block, Horton got to his feet. He was among the few who could. He had turned away to speak on his radio a moment before the blast, a lucky move that shielded him from the worst of it.

The explosion had kicked up a thick dust cloud. As it settled, Horton got a view of carnage. Most of the squad was down. Several were writhing in pain. Over the radio, he called to Captain Ryan Pike, the platoon's ground commander, who had remained thirty yards away, closer to where the helicopter had landed.

"We've got a mass casualty situation here," he said. Pike immediately summoned back the helicopter that had deposited them.

Thinking there could be more bombs inside the compound, Horton began pulling his wounded comrades away, closer to where he had been standing.

As soon as the first blast echoed across the valley, the platoon's principal medic, Specialist Bryan Anderson, who had been with the squirter team, ran toward the compound, his boots crunching over sand and rocks. His buddies needed him.

When Anderson reached the compound, he knelt beside a Ranger who had sustained serious shrapnel wounds to his legs and was crying out in agony. As Anderson started treating the soldier's wounds, the radio squawked with the reassuring news that the helicopter would be landing in sixty seconds.

Horton ordered anyone who could make his way to the landing zone to do so. One injured pair held on to each other and hobbled away, as if walking in a three-legged race. A few of the uninjured helped carry Block, who had been placed on a litter. But Horton needed help with the Ranger whom Anderson was treating. He called on the radio for assistance.

Among those listening was First Lieutenant Jennifer Moreno, twenty-five years old and the only woman on the assault team. A five-foot-tall, olive-skinned Army nurse from San Diego with an infectious smile, she had volunteered to deploy to Afghanistan with the Rangers. Her job was to interact with women the Rangers encountered on raids—to search them, question them, and determine if they were innocent relatives or participants in the insurgency. She and her fellow female Special Operations cultural-support specialists were closer to ground combat than almost every other American woman serving in Afghanistan.

Moreno, who had been standing near Pike, about thirty yards from the compound, heard Horton's call for an extra set of hands. She turned to Pike, who told her to stay put. He didn't know exactly what had happened at the compound. Were Ares 102 and the other insurgents still alive, waiting to attack? Where had the second blast come from?

But Horton needed help, so Moreno started to run toward him. Thirty yards. Twenty. Ten. Horton saw her closing in. He turned to get a count of the wounded who would be placed on the helicopter. Then he heard another explosion. He turned and gazed through the smoke to see that Moreno had been blown apart, killed instantly.

The helicopter landed. Block was hoisted aboard. Others straggled in on their own power. Remley didn't want to go, but his buddies insisted. He had suffered a debilitating concussion from the initial blast.

At that moment—just ninety seconds after Moreno had been felled—Sergeant Patrick Hawkins and Specialist Cody Patterson, two members of Horton's squad who had originally overshot the compound, found their way back to the site. They radioed Horton and began jogging toward him, ready to assist with the casualty evacuation.

Hawkins, who hailed from Carlisle, Pennsylvania, the home of the Army War College, had been a Ranger for three years and was on his fourth deployment to Afghanistan. He led one of Horton's gun teams. Patterson, from Philomath, Oregon, had joined the Rangers the previous November and was on his first combat tour.

As they approached from the east, they were engulfed by a thunderous blast. Three seconds later, there was another huge explosion. Both soldiers lay grievously wounded. Green smoke filled the air. It took Horton a second to figure out that the light sticks Hawkins carried had been blasted into the air.

Less than a minute later, yet one more earsplitting boom reverberated across the valley. Sergeant Joseph Peters, a special agent in the Army's Criminal Investigation Command, had been helping to move the wounded onto the helicopter. Like Moreno, he wasn't a Ranger, but he had become part of the First Platoon family. A native of Springfield, Missouri, he specialized in questioning detainees and gathering evidence at raid sites, helping the Joint Special Operations Command connect the dots to identify other Taliban leaders.

He, too, was down.

Holy shit, Horton thought. Until that moment, it hadn't been clear to him if insurgents had been shooting mortars at them. But seeing four comrades blown up in four minutes, with no other incoming blasts, he now knew they were in a minefield.

U.S. Army Field Manual 20-32 provides soldiers with unambiguous directives if they end up in a minefield:

> All personnel freeze.
> Do not help casualties because you could also become a casualty.

Medic Bryan Anderson knew the rules and the risks. He also knew that his buddies were down and that they needed his help. Remley was aboard the Chinook that was lifting off. The other member of the assault force with medical training, Tristan Windle, an Air Force Special Operations para–rescue man, was still with the squad pursuing the squirter.

Anderson had been blown back by the blasts that struck Patterson and Hawkins. The closer of the two men was just five yards away. Anderson's arm hurt and he felt woozy, but his limbs were intact. He crawled over to the Ranger he had been treating.

"Are you okay?" he asked.

"Yeah," he said. "I'm just a little dusty."

Anderson looked over at Hawkins, who was in far worse shape. He ran to his buddy. The mine had ripped the Ranger apart. His left arm was gone, as was his left leg. His abdomen was eviscerated. As Anderson tried to stem the bleeding from Hawkins's femoral artery, he searched for a pulse.

Seeing that Anderson needed help, another Ranger, Specialist Logan Howard, successfully braved the minefield, too. He put a tourniquet on what was left of Hawkins's left arm and held down a clump of gauze on his chest. Horton, who had so far managed to avoid serious injury, stepped over to assist with the left leg.

Anderson had performed first aid in arduous circumstances, but nothing had prepared him for this. He was working with night-vision goggles, smoke from the explosions and dust from the Chinook's whirling twin rotors had cut visibility to a few feet, and he was in a minefield. He sliced into Hawkins's neck and performed a tracheostomy, inserting a breathing tube. Hawkins took two shallow breaths. Then he stopped breathing.

Anderson didn't give himself time to grieve. He looked toward Patterson. A comrade was pulling him out of a hole carved out of the ground by one of the mines. Anderson knew at a glance there was nothing he could do. Patterson was the night's third American fatality.

There was another blast, Anderson remembered. *Someone else must be down,* he thought.

He couldn't see anything through his goggles, so he flipped on a white light on his helmet. Remaining stealthy was no longer a priority. He spotted Joe Peters, the criminal investigator. Both of his legs were gone, and his pelvis was shattered. He had an open head wound.

Anderson applied pressure to Peters's legs to stem the bleeding. As he reached for tourniquets, Staff Sergeant Zachary Skinner, a reconnaissance team leader who was among the few uninjured Rangers after the first two blasts, ran over to help. He, too, ignored the risks of the minefield. Skinner arrived safely and helped Anderson apply the tourniquets.

"I fucking need you, man," Horton radioed to Staff Sergeant Alexx Torres, the senior leader of the squad pursuing the squirter. The four blasts and the four downed comrades had left Horton at a loss. *Everything I try to do,* he thought, *it's not working.*

A minute later, Torres and members of his squad arrived.

"We can't move," Horton told him. "Too many fucking IEDs."

Torres saw that Horton's face was bleeding. He wanted to see if it was serious, but he told Horton that the only flashlight he had was on the scope of his M4 rifle.

"Fuck it," Horton said. "Do it."

Torres pointed his gun at Horton's face. "Just shrapnel wounds," Torres said. It was the best news Horton had had all night.

Among those who returned with Torres was Tristan Windle, the Air Force rescue specialist. They all trailed Sergeant Jeffery Dawson, the team's explosive-ordnance technician.

"What's going on?" Dawson asked Horton.

"There's shit everywhere," Horton said.

By then, Horton was beginning to feel helpless. The enemy seemed invisible.

Dawson was the bomb squad that night—the one guy among the thirty-three-man assault force with a metal detector and the know-how to defuse mines. He was on his first Special Operations deployment, and the challenge before him was unlike anything he'd experienced in combat or even in training.

Instead of allowing Windle to roll the dice as Anderson and Skinner had, Horton insisted that Dawson use his metal detector to quickly clear a thirty-yard path to the injured Peters. Because most of the makeshift bombs buried by the Taliban were made out of plastic jugs to reduce their metal content, and thus avoid detection, methodical sweeps and careful visual inspection for patches of disturbed earth were the best way to find IEDs, but Dawson didn't have the time. He hoped that his quick sweep would be enough.

Windle followed Dawson's path and then knelt down to help Anderson perform a tracheostomy on Peters. Anderson cut. Windle grabbed the tube. As they began to angle it into Peters's neck, another explosion blew them both over.

Fuck, thought Horton. *Again?*

Several minutes earlier, First Platoon's dog, Jani, had sniffed out the squirter, who had been hiding in a clump of underbrush in a gully. As Jani pounced, the squirter detonated a suicide vest, killing himself and the dog. None of the Rangers much liked Jani, a ferocious Belgian Malinois who had a tendency to bite them, but that night Jani had done his duty. Hoisting Jani over his shoulders, his handler, Corporal Joshua Hargis, was walking toward the compound when he saw that Peters was badly hurt. He was coming over to help, unaware of the minefield or of the safe path that Dawson had cleared, when he was blown into the air. Dawson, who had been standing nearby, was sprayed with shrapnel and suffered a ruptured eardrum.

Anderson left Windle to care for Peters and headed to Hargis, following Dawson's lead. Hargis had also lost his legs and sustained a shattered pelvis.

Hargis was bleeding out from what remained of his legs. With help from Dawson, Anderson straddled Hargis and put his knees— and as much pressure as he could muster—on the wounded Ranger's thighs to clamp down on the femoral arteries. Then Anderson fished around in his medical kit for his last two tourniquets. He strapped one around a thigh, which appeared to work. But the second one broke.

"Damn," he muttered to himself.

"Tourniquet!" he shouted. "I need a tourniquet!"

By then, Peters had died. Windle ran over to Anderson and Hargis, grabbing a tourniquet from another Ranger along the way. He helped Anderson get it on Hargis.

Anderson checked Hargis's wrist for a pulse. Nothing. When he checked Hargis's groin, he detected only a faint one. It was a sure sign that Hargis, who also had a collapsed lung, was going into shock.

Anderson resolved not to let this one die. He inserted a tube into Hargis's chest to relieve pressure around his heart from the collapsed lung. Then he pumped him with saline, freeze-dried blood plasma, and painkillers. To his astonishment, Hargis held on.

"Stay with me," Anderson told Hargis.

A few minutes later, he muttered, "You're going to make it."

At that point, Anderson was talking to himself as much as he was to Hargis.

Inside the operations center at the Kandahar airport, the most senior Ranger in the area, Lieutenant Colonel Patrick Ellis, was watching with mounting alarm a live video feed of the compound beamed down from a drone circling overhead. The grainy black-and-white infrared images showed what was unfolding on the ground. Every time a bomb detonated, the screen flashed white before turning black as smoke obscured the area. When it cleared, Ellis could see that more round black dots on the screen weren't moving.

As the screen depicted blast after blast, Ellis anxiously awaited a report from the ground commander. When Ellis heard the words "IED belt"—military-speak for minefield—he turned to Sergeant First Class Kerry Wertz, the senior noncommissioned officer in Second Platoon, who was in charge of that night's emergency response force.

"Get out there," Ellis said.

Wertz took twenty Rangers: two six-man squads, one gun team, two explosive-ordnance techs, a medic, and an air-support coordinator. Ten minutes after Ellis issued his order, they were airborne in a Chinook.

Because the pilot couldn't be sure his landing zone was free from mines, the helicopter didn't touch down. Instead, Wertz's men slid down ropes. The first to descend were the two bomb experts, Specialist Samuel Crockett and Sergeant First Class Moradda Tedesco. They scanned the landing area and, after pronouncing it safe, began clearing a path to Hargis and another wounded Ranger who had not been placed on the first medevac chopper.

Crockett and Tedesco used metal detectors and bright white lights to scan the ground. As they moved, they placed colored light sticks to their left and right so the soldiers behind them would be able to retrace the same path back to the landing zone.

By then, Dawson, their fellow explosive-ordnance expert, had identified three mines near Moreno's body and six other areas of disturbed earth that he believed concealed additional bombs. All seemed to be connected to a wire running through a drainage ditch.

It was part of a switch system that allowed people inside the compound to turn the minefield on and off.

If Dawson had been examining virgin terrain on which no mines had already exploded, he might have had a chance to defuse the bombs he detected one by one. But the soil was contaminated with bits of metal and dirt from previous explosions, and his detector was now almost useless. From a bomb-disposal perspective, Dawson deemed it the worst-case scenario.

As the emergency force neared the compound, the devastation they saw far exceeded what they had observed on the grainy drone feed. The black dots had turned into the bodies of their friends. And scattered across the landscape was something none of them had ever seen at a raid site: at least six American flags, blown out of pouches and ballistic vests, were unfurled on the ground as if in tribute to their dead teammates.

The newly arrived Rangers began to escort members of First Platoon back to the landing zone to await the next evacuation helicopter. When they reached Hargis, Anderson warned them to be careful.

"He's barely hanging on," he said. As they moved Hargis on a stretcher, Anderson stayed by his side.

Ten minutes later, they were on their way to the trauma center at the Kandahar airport. Hargis was on the floor of the Chinook, with Anderson kneeling next to him, along with the rest of First Platoon, save for Horton, Torres, and one other Ranger, who had remained to help the emergency force recover the bodies of Moreno, Hawkins, and Peters. Dawson, whom Torres ordered to leave for medical treatment, had already pulled Patterson's body to a safe area.

American troops, especially Rangers, try never to abandon their comrades on the battlefield, even if they are in a minefield. The Rangers' eleven-sentence creed is unambiguous on the point: "I will never leave a fallen comrade to fall into the hands of the enemy."

Bomb techs Crockett and Tedesco headed into the minefield. Crockett, who was on his first combat deployment, painstakingly cleared a ten-yard path to recover the remains of Hawkins and Jani. Tedesco moved in a different direction to collect Peters's body. Once that had been accomplished, Tedesco began moving toward Moreno.

As he neared her, his metal detector flashed repeatedly. He couldn't tell if metal debris on the ground or a mine below was setting it off. So he put his detector down and began to crawl, using his hands to dig and feel for any bombs beneath the surface. He eventually got to Moreno, cleared around her, and then widened the path back to the safe zone so she could be carried out. Then he guided two Rangers, Kyle Emmons and Derek Guay, to help him recover her body.

Emmons, a private first class, stood by her head. Sergeant Guay was at her shoulder. Tedesco was next to Guay. They began to lift.

And then, once again, an explosion.

Emmons was down. Tedesco was thrown back ten yards. Guay had also been thrown back a few yards but, amazingly, was still standing.

Crockett ran over. Once he reached the end of the area Tedesco had cleared, he began crawling to Emmons, whose right leg had been blown off. Upon reaching Emmons, he applied a tourniquet and dragged him to the safe area. Then Crockett went to fetch Guay, whose face was covered in blood. Again, he got on his hands and knees.

He made it five yards before triggering yet another mine. Crockett felt the ground give and saw a puff of dirt shoot a foot into the air. He waited. *Am I dead?* he wondered after a second. *I don't feel any pain.* He was, instead, the beneficiary of the only good fortune to befall the Rangers that night: the mine had failed to detonate fully.

Seeing that Crockett was unharmed, Guay called out to him. "Get your ass over here!"

Crockett, shifting his angle of approach, made it to Guay. After bringing him to safety, Crockett went back for Moreno's body. When he reached the end of the area he had determined to be free from mines, he used a cable with a hook to pull her body to him.

With Emmons and Guay injured, the Rangers no longer had enough stretchers to transport the dead, so they placed some of the bodies on ladders and covered them with the flags that were strewn about.

Finally, more than two hours after the first explosion, Wertz radioed the base. "Ready for exfil." Exfiltration. They were headed out of the minefield and back to their base.

When reports of the explosion that injured Emmons reached the Kandahar airport base, members of First Platoon who had already returned wanted to get back on a helicopter and return to the compound.

"They were furious they couldn't get out there," Anderson recalled.

Going to bed or watching television was unthinkable. There were no bars on base because alcohol was forbidden. And none of them felt up to working out in the gym. Instead, they swarmed the hospital. Some even donned latex gloves with the hope of helping the doctors treating their buddies, until a few insistent nurses forced them into the hallway.

Much of First Platoon returned to the hospital that afternoon with battalion commander Ellis and his boss, the leader of the overall Ranger regiment, Colonel Christopher Vanek. By then, Tom Block and Josh Hargis had been wheeled out of surgery. Both men lay unconscious in the intensive-care bay, breathing through ventilators, connected to an array of tubes and monitors, and covered with red, white, and blue quilts donated to the military by volunteer seamstresses. Doctors assured the Rangers that both men were going to survive.

Vanek carried two Purple Hearts. He pinned one on Block's blanket, then walked over to Hargis's bed and did the same. As Vanek affixed the gold-rimmed medal, which bears a profile of George Washington, Hargis began to struggle. The Rangers grew alarmed, and a nurse rushed over to calm him.

Ryan Pike, who had been the ground force commander, had been thinking about the long road Hargis faced after he left the trauma center: months in hospitals, more months in rehabilitation, learning to walk on prosthetic legs, finding a new line of work. His wife, Taylor, was pregnant. Becoming a father was now going to be even more daunting for him.

Hargis's movement on the bed worried Pike. *What's wrong? He was supposed to have been sedated.* Hargis had somehow managed to free his right arm. He brought his bandaged hand to his forehead in salute.

The soldiers froze, as did the nurses. Pike's arms erupted in goose bumps, and it was all he could do to hold back tears.

This is the most remarkable thing I have ever seen, he thought. He had never been prouder to be a Ranger. He knew his comrades had been seized by the same thought.

Galvanized, the able-bodied survivors in First Platoon asked to go on a raid that night, but Ellis demanded that they take some time to decompress. Finally, three days later, they were allowed out. For the next six weeks, until their return to Fort Benning, Georgia, the Rangers of First Platoon resumed their normal grueling schedule. When they suited up for missions in the ready room, nobody used Block's space, or Hargis's, or those belonging to their comrades who had returned home in caskets.

Everyone still took a flag.

Special Operations analysts concluded that none of the three insurgents at the compound was Ares 102, the intended target, but the revelation didn't bother members of First Platoon. They had taken three suicide bombers out of commission and disrupted plans for a major attack in Kandahar city.

"We lost four people," said First Sergeant Jesse Ragan, the senior noncommissioned officer in Bravo Company, "but we saved hundreds."

Six months after the raid, Rangers from Bravo Company stood shoulder to shoulder on the purple-curtained stage of an auditorium at Fort Benning. Their families sat before them, as did Rangers from other companies.

"You cannot help but be moved by the depth of their commitment to the Ranger mission and especially to one another," said Major General H. R. McMaster, the top commander at Benning. He bestowed a mint's worth of metal on them. The final tally of medals awarded for their actions that night made them one of the most decorated companies in Ranger history.

Forty-one Rangers received Purple Hearts.

Seven received Army Commendation Medals with valor designation.

Eight Bronze Stars with valor were awarded to those who survived: Staff Sergeant Aaron Arnold, Corporal Joshua Hargis, Staff Sergeant Kelan Horton, Specialist Logan Howard, Staff Sergeant Zachary Skinner, Sergeant First Class Moradda Tedesco, Sergeant First Class Kerry Wertz II, and Senior Airman Tristan Windle.

Posthumous Bronze Star medals with valor went to Lieutenant Jennifer Moreno, Sergeant Patrick Hawkins, Specialist Cody Patterson, and Sergeant Joseph Peters.

Specialist Samuel Crockett, the explosive-ordnance technician who crawled through the minefield to save Emmons and Guay, received the Silver Star.

Ranger commanders nominated Sergeant Jeffery Dawson and Bryan Anderson, who had been promoted to corporal after the raid, for the Distinguished Service Cross, the nation's second-highest decoration for combat valor.

"Anderson endured a total of seven IEDs or suicide vest blasts from a distance of no more than ten meters within the course of thirty minutes," his superiors wrote. "His utter disregard for his own safety to treat fellow comrades was astounding, and his efforts to deftly perform intricate and complicated medical procedures with minimal equipment were Herculean."

Dawson "consistently exposed himself" to bombs "to ensure safe passage for all teammates around the objective area," they wrote. "His expedient treatment directly contributed to saving the life of Corporal Hargis, and his focus on retrieving teammates from stranded positions ultimately saved theirs."

Their awards were not presented with the others at Benning. Service crosses are conferred only after senior military officials pore over after-action reports, witness statements, and accounts written by commanders. Those officials then submit a recommendation to the secretary of defense, who must approve the nomination. By the time Anderson's and Dawson's paperwork reached the secretary, Bravo Company had returned to Afghanistan for another deployment.

CHAPTER THREE

This Is What I Want to Do with My Life

In 2002, when Kellie McCoy became the first female engineer officer to join the Army's storied 307th Engineer Battalion, a former member of the unit wrote a message to one of her superiors that wound its way to her: "Ten thousand paratroopers are rolling over in their graves."

At the time, some in the 307th, a contingent of parachute-qualified soldiers who are trained in demolition and construction under fire, expressed similar feelings to McCoy's face. Though she was a captain, they refused to salute her as she walked through the motor pool in Fort Bragg, North Carolina. They'd stride past her naked on their way to the showers, some because they were simply ignoring her, others intent on provoking her. The following year, when the 307th headed to Iraq with the rest of the Eighty-Second Airborne Division as the war started, the battalion's commander didn't bring her. "I'll go to hell before she gets an Eighty-Second combat action patch," he told fellow officers.

Many of the military's gender barriers had been lifted by then—the Air Force allowed women to fly combat aircraft, and the Navy permitted them on combat ships—but the Army and the Marine Corps still barred women from ground combat positions. That meant the 307th and other combat engineer units had few slots open to female soldiers and even fewer for female officers such as

McCoy. Usually, they had to occupy administrative and support roles. Even when there were openings, combat commanders often shied from choosing women because they feared it would distract and disrupt the men they led. In the 1990s, several women had tried to join the 307th and had been rejected.

Army assignments are seldom a matter of choice. McCoy didn't ask to join the 307th but was selected because her professional report cards exceeded every other candidate's. She was incredulous about the opportunity—and apprehensive. She knew there would be a spotlight on her. "I'd have to do better just to be treated the same," she said.

KELLIE MCCOY

As a young girl, McCoy had never dreamed of joining the Army, let alone becoming a trailblazing female officer. The eldest of four siblings raised in St. Louis—her father was a paramedic, her mother a nurse—she didn't love sports, long hikes, shooting, or many of the other passions that push kids toward the Army. She preferred to study and read.

At eight, she persuaded her mother to enroll her in a Mandarin Chinese language class at the local college. When she was in the sixth grade, she took algebra classes. She skipped seventh grade. The following year, her parents moved so she could attend a high school with International Baccalaureate courses, where she spent her lunch breaks in the library, devouring biographies and histories.

She wanted to go to college, but she knew that her parents couldn't afford to foot the bill. Even though she had been awarded a National Merit Scholarship, she would have to receive other assistance or take out the necessary loans. Then she happened to see a television show about a teenage girl who applies to the Air Force Academy. Intrigued, she went to the library the next day and read all she could about service academies. She decided to apply to the Air Force's and the Army's and sought the required nominations from her congressman, Richard Gephardt. His office called and told her she had to choose between them. She had just devoured an epic history of West Point's class of 1966, Rick Atkinson's *The Long Gray Line,* and had concluded that the institution, which the book described as "a preserve of the nation's values," was the place she wanted to be.

She headed to West Point that fall. She didn't sweat the stuff that trips up most cadets—the academic course load of her rigorous math major or even the rote memorization of school trivia, menus in the dining hall, and headlines from each day's *New York Times.* But other things vexed her. She had no idea how to shine shoes. She fumbled through the obstacle course. She hated road marches. She had never touched a gun in her life. And on the first day, when the cadet in the red sash, to whom each "firstie" had to report, barked out an order, she stood flummoxed.

"Post!"

"Sir, I do not understand."

He repeated his directive to depart.

"Sir, I do not understand."

She worked to address her shortcomings, practicing the obstacle course and brushing up on Army lingo. She coxswained the women's crew team, finding the perfect leadership role for a ninety-eight-pound teenager. At her commencement in 1996, her academic ranking was among the top 5 percent in her class. The following day, she married a classmate in the West Point chapel, and they soon moved to Germany, where he served as an armor officer and she as an engineer platoon commander.

It was her first taste of Army life, and she loved it. As a newly minted second lieutenant, she had forty soldiers under her command. Construction jobs and training exercises took them across eastern Europe and the Balkans, where she helped to build Camp Bondsteel, the large American base in Kosovo. But the travel and the long hours at work, even when on base, strained her marriage. When their deployments ended three and a half years later and she and her husband returned to the United States, they had an amicable divorce. She went off to Fort Leonard Wood, Missouri, to take an engineer-officer course necessary for promotion to captain and then stuck around for six more months to pick up a master's degree in environmental engineering.

Then she headed to Fort Bragg. Her first day of work there had been September 11, 2001. The attacks on New York and Washington gave her new purpose: She didn't just want to oversee the assembly of bridges and buildings in safe, rear-echelon places; she needed to help in the theaters of war. But she also didn't believe in bashing through the Army's glass ceiling with a sledgehammer. She thought that ceiling needed to be dismantled methodically, one pane at a time.

When McCoy joined the 307th at Bragg, she threw her five-foot frame into demonstrating that she could compete with the boys. Donning coveralls, she turned wrenches with her men in the vehicle maintenance yard. Then she set out to become a jumpmaster, which required a detailed understanding of parachuting and completion of at least a dozen airborne drops. She also devoted herself to the task of equipment maintenance, putting in longer hours than almost anyone else in the battalion.

She was a soldier, but no culture warrior. She brushed off most of the mistreatment she experienced, chalking it up to ignorance and testosterone, not actual malice. When she did confront soldiers over their behavior toward her, she talked to them discreetly. Respect followed. Soon after the battalion returned from its first foray in Iraq—the one from which she had been excluded—she was promoted to command the battalion's headquarters company. Her new assignment included being in charge of a platoon of combat engineers—the Army calls them sappers—a job closed off to women. She would become one of the first female officers to command ground combat troops, but in one of the oddities of the modern Army, she would be ordering soldiers to perform duties that she herself was barred from.

Within weeks, she heard that the Eighty-Second Airborne Division would head back to Iraq in three months. Based on the first deployment, she figured she and her company would be left behind again. Nonetheless, she put her soldiers through the same rigorous training regimen that other Eighty-Second Airborne troops were undergoing, including exercises that headquarters companies in engineering battalions normally did not attempt. Among them was a live-fire exercise that required her soldiers to drive a convoy through an enemy ambush. A month later, the commanding general of the Eighty-Second disabused McCoy of her stay-at-home assumptions. "Everyone's going," he said.

=★=

Three days after she arrived in Iraq, McCoy drove off the giant base that served as the Eighty-Second Airborne's headquarters. In other wars, commanders of headquarters engineer companies did not usually travel "outside the wire"—their job was to maintain and secure the headquarters base. But in Iraq, because the division was spread across a vast swath of the country's western desert, McCoy had been asked to help construct and operate a dozen different outposts. To facilitate that mission, her company had been split. Half the soldiers under her command—about ninety—were stationed twenty miles away at the al-Taqaddum Air Base near Fallujah. She was going to check on them.

As her four-vehicle convoy departed, she instructed her driver to pull their Humvee into the second position in the column. Her daily intelligence reports stated that insurgents triggering roadside bombs most commonly targeted the second vehicle. They didn't want to risk blowing too early if they aimed for the first, and they didn't want to allow everyone else to drive away if they hit the end of the convoy. *This is where I need to be,* she thought.

Compared with the hulking trucks the military would begin to procure a few years later, with inch-thick steel plates, bulletproof glass, and satellite-linked communications systems, McCoy's convoy looked like an Army version of a *Beverly Hillbillies* caravan: two Humvees with no doors, no armor plating, and no long-distance radios; and two five-ton trucks, also bereft of any protection from bullets and bombs. Only one of the vehicles—the last truck in the column—had a mounted weapon. It was the Army's smallest machine gun.

The forty-five-minute drive to al-Taqaddum was uneventful, which was unsurprising. It was September 2003, and the Iraqi insurgency was in its infancy. Daily attacks on American troops, more harassing than horrific, could be counted on a single hand. McCoy met with her soldiers and discussed plans for the coming week with her first sergeant, the company's top noncommissioned officer. And then it was time to head back to the headquarters base. McCoy and eleven other soldiers, in the same four vehicles, retraced their path along Highway 10 in the late afternoon.

As they neared the city of Ramadi, traffic thinned. McCoy hadn't been in Iraq long enough to find that odd. Then an oncoming car flashed its headlights at other drivers. That she understood. It was a signal to civilians on the road to steer clear of the Americans.

We need to stop the convoy, McCoy thought. *Now!*

She reached toward the center console to grab the radio handset.

BOOM!

A 155-millimeter artillery shell, buried in a dirt berm on the right side of the road, exploded in front of her Humvee, kicking up a blinding cloud of smoke and debris but leaving the occupants unscathed. Her driver, Zachary Brombacher, a private first class, immediately yanked the steering wheel to the left, worried there might be more explosions. The force of the turn hurled McCoy to the right, out the doorless side. She grabbed on to the rearview mirror, and a communications specialist in the seat behind her reached over and pulled her back inside the vehicle by the strap on her flak vest.

Just as Brombacher straightened out the Humvee on the far left side of the roadway, a blast hit the truck leading the convoy. Then there was a detonation to the rear. And another.

McCoy told Brombacher to drive toward the truck ahead, which had ground to a halt in the road. As they pushed forward, she saw a piece of metal the size of a soda can fly across the road a few yards in front of her Humvee.

I wonder what that is.

It struck the ground to the side of the road and exploded.

"RPG," she shouted. She'd never seen a rocket-propelled grenade before, but she recognized it from her training. Then she heard the crackle of gunfire from the other side of the road. She realized that the roadside bombs were only the opening act. She and her soldiers were being ambushed and were fenced-in prey. The attack, among the most sophisticated at that point in the war, consisted of daisy-chained artillery rounds, intended to take out an entire convoy.

She began to fire at the insurgents on the right side with her M4 carbine. The soldier behind her, the one who had saved her from falling out, also began shooting. Brombacher kept his hands on the wheel. The soldier in the rear left seat was a chaplain's assistant.

When they reached the truck, she saw that the three occupants, who were returning fire and trying to fend off attacks on both sides of the road, had been walloped by the blasts. Blood poured from the ears of the sergeant in charge of the truck. A younger soldier riding in the back had been plastered with shrapnel. As McCoy and the others in her Humvee got out to help, a pair of guerrillas ran up to the Humvee and began shooting at close range. The Americans returned a hail of gunfire, killing both.

McCoy grabbed the injured soldiers, one at a time, and brought them back to her Humvee. She directed the truck's driver to pull out the radios, maps, and other sensitive items from the damaged truck and join them in her vehicle, all the while popping off rounds at the insurgents across the berm.

As soon as she had packed the three men from the truck into her Humvee and climbed back into the front seat, a trio of insurgents charged toward her side of the vehicle, firing as they ran. The lessons of the convoy-ambush exercise McCoy had run her soldiers through at Bragg kicked in.

The two insurgents in the lead were no more than twenty-five yards away—so close that she could see their eyes and the curved clips of their AK-47 assault rifles. She aimed her M4 at one and pulled the trigger, unleashing a volley of 5.56-millimeter rounds. He dropped. Then she took out the other one.

As she reached down to swap out her empty ammunition clip for a full one, another fighter, carrying an RPG, sprinted toward them. McCoy remembered that the soldier behind her had an M203 grenade launcher affixed to his rifle.

"Hey, you got any rounds for that thing?" she shouted. When he said he did, she told him to take aim at the RPG-wielding assailant before he pulverized their Humvee. The soldier fired, and the insurgent was blown apart.

With those three attackers dead, McCoy ordered Brombacher to turn around and drive toward the two rear vehicles in the convoy. The Humvee behind hers looked fine, but the truck at the end of the column had been struck by an RPG and appeared immobilized. The five soldiers back there were still under fire. When McCoy neared, she was amazed that the three soldiers who had been riding in the truck had escaped with only minor shrapnel wounds. Then she saw that the soldier assigned to the machine gun mounted on the roof was crouched behind the vehicle.

"Get on the gun!" she ordered. He complied, and the resulting fusillade from his belt-fed weapon forced the last few insurgents to flee.

Worried that the assailants might try to regroup, McCoy told the truck's occupants to jump into the second Humvee. Then both vehicles took off toward the headquarters base. As they rolled, McCoy picked up her radio handset to summon a quick-response force to aid her wounded soldiers and recover the trucks.

"All-American Main, this is Stick Six," she said.

No answer.

"All-American Main, this is Stick Six," she repeated.

Still no answer.

They must have hit the radio, she concluded. *We're on our own.*

A few minutes later, the second Humvee sputtered and stopped. It, too, had been hit in the ambush. Because they weren't far from the site of the attack, McCoy didn't want to pause to make repairs. But she wasn't sure if her radio calls for assistance had been received.

She got out and began pulling boxes of food and water from the tailgate of her own vehicle and tossing them onto the road. "Let's clear everything out," she said. A folding picnic chair, which had been carried all the way from North Carolina by one of the soldiers, joined the pile of supplies on the asphalt. The five soldiers in the broken Humvee watched.

She pointed to her vehicle, which had been stuffed with seven soldiers.

"Everybody in!"

Six soldiers jumped in the rear, their legs dangling off the sides. Six squeezed into the passenger compartment. McCoy sat on top of the radio, wedging her petite body into the console between the driver and the front passenger seat.

"Let's haul ass," she told Brombacher. When they reached the base, he drove straight to the first-aid station. After her men had been triaged, McCoy strode over to the command post to inform them of the attack. By then, however, they knew. CNN was airing footage of her trucks, which had been set on fire.

So this is what it's going to be like for the rest of our time here, she thought as she walked back to her company's corner of the base. She met with her soldiers to hear their reactions to the attack and talk about how they could respond differently the next time. Before allowing them to get some much-needed rest, she told them that they'd be going out again the following day.

"I used to get my chops busted for driving a female commander," Brombacher said. "After the attack, nobody said anything."

=★=

The rest of McCoy's deployment hewed to her prediction: more attacks, more injuries, more heart-fibrillating journeys along hostile roads. A suicide bomber penetrated the headquarters base and detonated a car filled with explosives. A quarter of her company received Purple Hearts. Two of her men returned home in flag-draped caskets.

McCoy had arrived in Iraq thinking that she would leave the Army upon her return to America. She had fulfilled her post–West Point commitment and was keen to pursue another graduate degree or put her math and engineering skills to use in the private sector. Her company's responsibilities were prosaic—set up combat outposts, deliver the mail, replace the glass on broken windows after bomb blasts, help the Iraqis repair downed electric power lines. None of it taxed her.

She also wasn't someone who relished the privation of war-zone life. She had brought a hair dryer to Iraq, and she built a gravity-fed shower that used water from the Euphrates River.

But each day she spent at war, she fell a little more in love with the challenge of serving as an officer, overseeing the work of 180 soldiers, ensuring their safety, deciding how to allocate precious engineering resources, and participating in Iraq's reconstruction. Halfway through her deployment, her future fell into place in her head. Money didn't matter to her—she had been raised frugally—and she didn't have an entrepreneurial bent. She wanted to serve others, and she actually liked the Army, despite its often-maddening bureaucracy.

This is what I want to do with my life, she thought.

When she returned to Fort Bragg in the spring of 2004, she received two surprises. One was an award for her actions during the ambush: a Bronze Star with a valor commendation, a first for a woman in the Eighty-Second Airborne. "McCoy willingly and repeatedly took action to gather up her soldiers under enemy fire and direct fire at the enemy," the award citation read. "Her actions inspired her men to accomplish the mission and saved the lives of her fellow soldiers."

The second was a job offer. While in Iraq, she used a small boat to ferry supplies across the Euphrates to a covert encampment used by members of the Delta Force, the Army's most elite commandos. Her ingenuity in fixing up their camp had so impressed the all-male D-Boys that a senior noncommissioned officer in the unit recommended her for the position of task force engineer.

McCoy spent two and a half years with Delta. Some of it was at Bragg, where she had the distinctly unsexy task of maintaining the unit's facilities. But she also was asked to help design training exercises for the commandos, which was unlike anything she had done previously. For one drill, she told them, "I'm going to lease an old school and let you guys blow it up."

Jumping out of planes with the Delta guys made her Eighty-Second Airborne training seem like playground exercises. The commandos conducted high-altitude jumps that required oxygen tanks and steel nerves. McCoy, who flew through the air strapped to a Delta soldier, found it exhilarating.

When she wasn't helping them train, she accompanied them to Iraq for two tours, often the only woman in the Delta fraternity. While there, she was a jack-of-all-trades, serving as their plumber, electrician, and carpenter. She strung data cables and unclogged toilets. She went wherever she was needed and did whatever the commandos asked. She once spent two months retrofitting a safe house in western Iraq, sleeping on the floor of the pantry next to sacks of potatoes. It suited her fine—except for when the D-Boys opened the door in the wee hours of the morning, looking for snacks after returning from raids.

McCoy used her Delta assignment as a form of graduate school in elite warfare. Every morning, Lieutenant General Stanley McChrystal, who ran the Joint Special Operations Command, chaired a battle update briefing, where McCoy learned about the strategy and tactics Special Operations forces were using to combat insurgents. Instead of spending her free time watching movies, she would sit in the command center, watching footage from Predator drones—then a new addition to the American air arsenal—which gave her a preview of technologies that would trickle down to the conventional Army five years later.

McCoy called herself a "gap filler." If the Delta guys ever needed a hand, she volunteered, even to pick up a squawking radio in the command center. One night, the voice on the other end was a commando asking for a helicopter exfiltration from a raid site. As she began to respond, she realized that she didn't have a call sign— nobody expected the facilities engineer to be on the radio—so she simply announced herself by saying, "This is Kellie." The Delta guys loved it. From that day on, all the guys called her Kellie. In any other part of the Army, for a non-officer to address her as anything other than Captain McCoy would have been a sign of disrespect. In the Delta world, however, it meant that she was now a member of the club.

After her Delta assignment, the Army promoted McCoy to major and selected her to attend the Command and General Staff College at Fort Leavenworth, Kansas, where promising young officers are groomed for more senior leadership roles. Many soldiers treat their stint there as a sabbatical year, free from the rigors of deployment and training, a time to sleep late and take long weekend trips. Not McCoy, even though she had been running at a sprint since 2001 and had spent her monthlong break after Delta walking five hundred miles along the Camino de Santiago, a pilgrimage path across Spain. She took extra classes—Russian history, just for fun— and elected to write a thesis to obtain a second master's degree. She researched and wrote about transitional governments after conflicts, concluding with a blistering critique of American efforts during her first tour in Iraq.

While she was at Leavenworth, she heard that one of the Eighty-Second's brigades needed a staff engineer for its next deployment to Iraq. After all of the time she had already spent in Iraq, she had her pick of low-key assignments in the United States. But they didn't appeal to her. Iraq did. She finished her course work and her thesis a few weeks ahead of schedule and drove back to Fort Bragg to start training with the brigade. As soon as she arrived, she got a phone call ordering her to report back to Leavenworth. She needed to attend the college's graduation, she was told, because she would be receiving the General George C. Marshall Award, given to the top student in each year's class. David Petraeus, the former four-star general who commanded the Iraq and Afghanistan wars, was among the previous recipients.

When she arrived in Baghdad in 2008, her engineering challenge no longer involved erecting bases and moving the mail. It was route clearance: keeping roads used by American troops free from IEDs, which had become far more accurate and deadly since the ambush on her convoy nearly six years earlier. Her principal worry was an Iranian-designed roadside bomb that could shoot a disk of molten steel through even the toughest American trucks, killing the occupants. The military was spending billions of dollars a year to develop ways to detect the bombs, but nothing was as effective as a pair of well-trained eyes. Route-clearance engineers tried to spot piles of trash and dirt that contained the bombs and then dismantle them before insurgents could trigger the fuse. But often the explosives were too well concealed. Engineers were hit by blasts far more frequently than other troops. "It was a god-awful deployment for them," McCoy said.

She decided which roads the engineers would examine, and when, a responsibility that weighed on her. If the engineers weren't scanning for threats, she knew that increased the risk for other American units, but still she felt the burden. To demonstrate her solidarity, she visited every engineer unit in the brigade. All of them welcomed her, and some brought her along on patrols, even though Army regulations did not permit her to serve in their roles. Women were still not allowed to be sappers.

Eighteen months after McCoy returned from Baghdad, she was back at war—in Kandahar. Major General James Huggins, who had been awed by her moxie in Iraq in 2003, asked her to be his executive officer while he served as the top U.S. and NATO commander in southern Afghanistan. McCoy traveled everywhere with Huggins and sat in on almost all of his meetings, from sessions with Afghan tribal chiefs to a surprise visit from the British prime minister, David Cameron. She fulfilled the role of an aide—taking notes, preparing memos, and accompanying Huggins to the hospital as he pinned Purple Hearts on every wounded trooper—but she also served as his de facto strategic adviser, helping him refine the fight against the Taliban and transition responsibility for security to the Afghans. "There wasn't anything she couldn't do," Huggins recalled.

Nor was there much she wouldn't do. On a trip to a tiny base north of Kandahar city, Huggins returned from walking around with a Special Forces commander to find McCoy waist-deep in mud, helping soldiers fix a broken water pump. "She has no pretensions," he said. "She was just as comfortable in the muck as she was talking to General [John] Allen," then the top American commander in Afghanistan.

McCoy's year in Kandahar led to yet another promotion—to lieutenant colonel—and a coveted assignment: in the summer of 2014, she assumed command of an engineer battalion with the

Tenth Mountain Division at Fort Drum, New York. The battalion, comprising nearly eight hundred soldiers, is part of an Army brigade combat team, making her one of the first women to command such a large unit of combat-focused forces.

Before she took charge of the battalion, she insisted on one more deployment. Her Army friends thought she was crazy, but they also knew it was classic Kellie: The Tenth Mountain headquarters was heading to Afghanistan in 2013, and she figured it would be a good chance to get to know soldiers in the division. So she volunteered to serve as the division's chief of plans.

Staff planning jobs can often be dull and thankless assignments, but she was given the responsibility of crafting the departure of American troops from eastern Afghanistan. Determinations about when to close bases, where to move troops, and how to remove equipment fell to her and her team. For the first five months of 2014, however, McCoy was operating without a key piece of information: President Obama had not decided how many troops would remain in Afghanistan after December 31, 2014.

McCoy made an educated guess—ten thousand—and designed her plans around that number. Her superiors didn't question her prediction. They figured the woman who as a young girl had studied algebra while her classmates were still learning long division knew her numbers.

They were right. That May, the president announced that 9,800 U.S. troops would stay.

By the Army's measure, McCoy was a hero for a day, perhaps just for an hour, as she repelled the 2003 ambush, killed a pair of insurgents, and rescued her soldiers. Her true valor, however, is evident in her career of service, still in its prime: grueling combat deployments, a refusal to accept the easy jobs, a series of trailblazing charges into terrain long off-limits to female soldiers. She is far from the only service member to have worked so tirelessly since September 11, 2001. Hundreds of others have spent more than four years in the war zones. But her enthusiasm to return to the battle zones again and again, in roles that included maintenance worker, company commander, and general's aide, over a dozen years, in both Iraq and Afghanistan, placed her among a select few officers. For McCoy, the measure of her devotion to the nation involved more than fifteen hundred days at war, with nearly every waking hour of each day focused on leading, supporting, and mentoring her fellow soldiers.

CHAPTER FOUR

The Last Line of Defense

The tanker truck turned onto the bumpy dirt driveway without hesitation or haste, as if the driver had been down the road to Joint Security Station Nasser dozens of times on his morning rounds. From the other end of the fifty-yard-long driveway, next to the metal gate that opened into an Iraqi police station, it was impossible to tell what was in the silver cylinder affixed to an aquamarine chassis—perhaps water or kerosene, or room for the effluent that had to be vacuumed from plastic-walled portable toilets.

Two Iraqi policemen stood guard at the mouth of the driveway. One motioned for the driver to stop, squeezing the fingers on his right hand together and pointing them upward. He wanted to check the driver's papers and ask about the contents of the tank. The truck kept rolling. The policemen picked up their AK-47 rifles and squeezed off a few rounds, but the cab had passed them. Their bullets ricocheted off the truck's steel frame.

The police station at the end of the driveway had been established a year earlier by American forces as part of a new war strategy. U.S. commanders believed that if Iraqi policemen were out patrolling, inspecting vehicles, and responding to requests for help, their presence would reassure the civilian population and make it more difficult for insurgents to operate. The station, situated between a mosque and a private home, was one of more than a dozen new neighborhood outposts in Ramadi, a sand-swept city along the Euphrates River that had long been one of the most dangerous places in Iraq.

The square compound behind the front gate contained two cinder-block buildings, latrines, a row of pickup trucks, and a few corrugated-metal shipping containers. One of the buildings was originally intended to house the policemen, but most of them went home in the evenings, so it had become a nap and recreation facility and a daytime operations center. The other building was home to the men who ensured the Iraqi cops left their base every day and went on patrol: a reinforced squad of American Marines.

There were usually about sixteen Marines at the station. But on this morning—April 22, 2008—there were thirty-five, plus a score of Iraqi cops. A new squad, fresh from the United States, had arrived the day before to relieve the Marines who had been there for seven months and were due to head home in three days.

It was just after seven in the morning, and several Marines were still asleep. Others were brushing their teeth. A few began to rummage through ration bags for breakfast. Thirty-three of the Marines were inside the station. The other two stood next to the gate in a guard post constructed of plywood and sandbags.

Jonathan Yale, a twenty-one-year-old corporal, who was getting ready to depart.

Jordan Haerter, a nineteen-year-old lance corporal, who had just arrived.

They had met for the first time three hours before, when they had both volunteered to man the guard post at the gate, Entry Control Point One.

Yale had spent the morning explaining the routine at ECP One to Haerter. If a vehicle approached, Marines were not to open fire immediately. To minimize civilian casualties, they had to follow "escalation of force" procedures. First wave an orange flag. If the

JONATHAN YALE, LEFT, AND JORDAN HAERTER

car doesn't stop, flash a bright light at the driver. If that doesn't work, then fire a few rounds—but at the engine block. If all that fails, then—and only then—is deadly force authorized.

That force could be delivered only with a light machine gun. At one time, Yale's squad had had a bigger gun there, but an Iraqi cop had used it to strafe the neighboring mosque. The Marines couldn't tell if it was an accident or intentional. Either way, the big gun was replaced with a smaller one.

At six in the morning, Benjamin Tupaj, a fellow lance corporal in Haerter's squad, had radioed the duo. Want some coffee? Need some food? Haerter declined. It was his first day at work in a war zone. He was too excited to need any caffeine, but he wanted an extra battery for his radio. Tupaj brought him one.

A half hour later, Yale's squad leader, Sergeant Gerald Foxx, was awakened by a fellow Marine who reported that most of the Iraqi policemen assigned to the day shift had not arrived as scheduled. Foxx sighed. He wasn't worried—the cops were a notoriously lazy bunch. "Let's get a patrol out there to find these guys," he said.

As Foxx was beginning his day, Haerter's team leader, Lance Corporal Corey Teague, got on the radio with a warning to Haerter.

Most attacks in Iraq, he said, occur between daybreak and dawn. "Be watchful," he said. "Be careful."

"Roger that," Haerter said. "Good to go."

Thirty minutes later, the tank truck turned off the four-lane main drag the Marines called Route Michigan and headed down the driveway. Haerter and Yale went through the escalation-of-force procedures. The truck kept coming, weaving through three concrete barriers placed in a zigzag pattern along the driveway to prevent oncoming vehicles from traveling too fast. Even moving at a low speed, however, the truck was massive enough that it would be able to knock over the gate.

Haerter and Yale shot at the truck's grille. The driver didn't stop. So the two Marines aimed at the windshield and opened fire. Yale on the light machine gun, Haerter with his M16 rifle, standing shoulder to shoulder, letting fly as many rounds as they could.

There was no hesitation, no call over the radio asking, "What should we do?"

As the shots rang out, an Iraqi policeman sitting inside the gate on a plastic chair peered through the gap in the wall. When he saw the truck, he took off running into the compound as fast as he could move.

Haerter and Yale stood their ground, firing away.

In his first three years of high school, Jordan Haerter spent all of his spare time in his room, glued to his computer, playing video games. The *Call of Duty* series, in which players shoot their way through enemy terrain, was his favorite. He jousted with fellow enthusiasts around the world. If he lost, from across the house his mother would hear him screaming at his computer. More often, though, he racked up the highest score.

Jordan had played Little League and camped with the Boy Scouts, but sitting in his room all the time, he grew into a stocky teenager. He didn't join organized sports at his high school in Sag Harbor, a cozy hamlet on New York's Long Island, and he shied away from summertime volleyball games on the nearby beach. "He wasn't a gung-ho kid," recalled his father, Chris Haerter. "If he had to go from Point A to B, he'd walk, not run."

For his thirteenth birthday, Chris paid for a flying lesson for Jordan. The fee, pocket change for many of their neighbors in the opulent Hamptons, was a splurge for Chris, who owns a water-treatment company. Though he was divorced from Jordan's mother, JoAnn Lyles, they both worked hard to provide their son with a comfortable life.

Jordan's fingers, so deft on the keyboard, quickly took to the switches and levers in the cockpit. Soon after turning sixteen, and before he knew how to drive a car, he came home with the back of his T-shirt cut out. When Chris asked about it, Jordan proudly explained that his fellow pilots had torn the fabric to celebrate his first solo flight.

In the tenth grade, with his parents in attendance, Jordan announced to his high school career counselor that he wanted to join the Marine Corps. Although he had the grades to get into college, where he could have signed up for an ROTC program, he wanted to enlist as soon as he was done with high school.

His parents were stunned but not entirely surprised. In late August 2001, Jordan had visited Manhattan with a cousin and traveled to the top of the World Trade Center. The terrorist attack that felled the towers a few weeks later scarred him deeply. It wasn't something he talked about with friends, but his parents knew. "Things always were black or white for him," his mother said. "He believed justice needed to be served."

By the time Jordan met with the counselor, however, it was 2004, and America's gun sights were aimed at Iraq. That's where Jordan would be sent if he joined, and it was getting more hazardous by the day. When the meeting with the counselor was over, Chris asked his son, who was enamored of flying, why he didn't want to join the Air Force, which he figured would be safer. Flying was fun, Jordan replied, but he had mastered it. Now it was time for the next thing. The Marines, he told his father, "are the biggest challenge." His parents didn't try to talk him out of it.

When Jordan entered his senior year, he dealt them another surprise. Instead of banging away at his computer keyboard, he developed a new afternoon routine: he would drive for an hour to the nearest Marine recruiting station, where he ran, performed calisthenics, and joined in impromptu football games with fellow recruits. Over the course of the year, his waist shrank ten inches. He became the sort of kid who would run from A to B.

Because Jordan would be graduating at seventeen, his parents had to sign papers allowing him to enlist. "I could have gone one of two ways: I could have refused to sign and know that he would do it on his own at eighteen, or I could support him," his father said. "I didn't want there to be any possibility of him going to war thinking we weren't fully supportive of his decision to join."

Jordan graduated from the Corps' grueling thirteen-week boot camp at Parris Island, South Carolina, in December 2006. As he marched across the parade ground clad, like hundreds of his fellow privates, in an olive-green coat and dress hat, his father struggled to spot him. When he saw his boy—his deep-set eyes, pointy nose, and thin, pursed lips—earlier doubts gave way to pride. And fear. His son had developed the mental and physical toughness to be a Marine. But in those days, becoming a Marine, particularly an infantryman, as Jordan wanted to be, was dangerous business. Chris and JoAnn never voiced their concerns to Jordan. Both had concluded independently that if their son was to face a war, he needed strong, supportive parents.

Next it was off to the Marines' School of Infantry and then to a combat unit. Now eighteen, Jordan was sent to Camp Lejeune, North Carolina, and assigned to the First Battalion, Ninth Marines. Its nickname, bestowed as a threat by the North Vietnamese leader Ho Chi Minh and appropriated by the Marines with relish, was "the Walking Dead."

Many of Jordan's fellow junior Marines were loud and boisterous, oozing bravado. They'd train hard during the day and party even harder at night in the bars and strip clubs outside the base. Not Jordan. He seldom joined in the banter and boastful chatter of his buddies. His team leader never had to tell him to do anything twice. He took notes to remember crucial information and asked pertinent questions. Instead of fooling around at Lejeune on weekends, he would jump into his Dodge pickup and drive for eleven hours to Sag Harbor to see his parents and his girlfriend, Nicole Jonat.

The night before he shipped out to Iraq, he sent her a seven-second video he recorded while lying in his bunk. "I love you," he said. He blew a kiss, waved, and gave her a thumbs-up.

Jon Yale had forged a very different path to ECP One that morning. He was raised in a one-street Virginia farming town thirty-two miles from where Robert E. Lee surrendered. He was half-black, half-white. He had wanted to join the Air Force, but ear and nose ailments prevented him from flying.

In high school, he was the quick-with-a-joke class clown. He formed a skateboarding club, participated in an antidrug advocacy program, and joined the drama club, once playing three different characters in a single performance, including an elderly woman, complete with wig, skirt, and makeup. And he was a cheerleader. At

football games, dressed in a uniform, he shouted through a mega-
phone and jumped around on the sidelines. "He was one of a kind,"
his mother, Rebecca Yale, said. "When God created him, he broke
the mold."

Rebecca gave birth to him when she was seventeen and raised
him by herself, along with a daughter, Tammy, who arrived when
Jon was five. His father was a once-every-few-years visitor, though
he lived a half hour away. Rebecca hailed from a military family—
her father had been in the Navy, and two of her uncles had been
soldiers—but she had never expected Jon to enlist. He seemed too
fun-loving to spend his days drilling. But during his senior year in
high school, he drove for an hour and a half to meet with a Marine
recruiter. When he told his mother, she urged him to reconsider.
"You're my only boy," she said. He was insistent. "That's where I
need to be," he told her. "I need to make a difference."

She was worried he'd be shipped off to Iraq. He was noncha-
lant. "I'm going to go over there, I'm going to kick some ass, and
then I'm coming home."

After boot camp, he came home for a brief holiday before heading to infantry school. "That was fun," he told the sergeant who
gave him a ride. "Can I do it again?"

A few months after Jon finished infantry training and moved to
Camp Lejeune, Rebecca split with Tammy's father. When she told
Jon that she was looking for a new place to live, he made an offer
that few young Marines would: "Mom, pack your and Tammy's
stuff and come on down here."

He didn't mean the nearby town. He meant the base. He
requested—and received—an apartment for families. It helped
his application that Jon was married—on paper. He and a classmate had gotten hitched in the spring of his senior year in high
school. The relationship dissolved after a week, but neither of them

had bothered to petition the court for a divorce. Jon earned about twenty-three thousand dollars a year as a lance corporal, the third-lowest rank in the Corps. He used all of his paycheck to support his mother and sister.

He was assigned to the Second Battalion of the Eighth Marine Regiment, which departed for Iraq in October 2007. His platoon, part of the battalion's weapons company, was assigned to set up a police station in eastern Ramadi and mentor Iraqi officers. This task was part of an effort to capitalize on security improvements after tribal leaders earlier that year had decided to forsake al-Qaeda and cast their lot with the new Iraqi government. Until a few months earlier, Ramadi had been racked by intense insurgent attacks. By the time Yale's battalion arrived, many of those who had been fighting the Americans were willing to work with them. Some even agreed to serve as policemen. For Yale and his fellow Marines, the change was exciting. They were going to help turn Iraq around.

In late 2007, about halfway through their seven-month deployment, Yale was up for promotion to corporal. All he needed was the signature of the weapons company's top noncommissioned officer, First Sergeant Darrell Rowe. When word filtered out to members of Yale's platoon, some of them approached Rowe to try to dissuade him from approving the promotion. "They said he wasn't the fastest, he wasn't the best shooter," Rowe recalled. But Yale had his paperwork in order, had completed the necessary courses, and had passed his fitness test. Rowe ignored the critics and signed off. He had a feeling about Yale. *This guy is going to be a very good Marine.*

Joint Security Station Nasser had none of the amenities of the large bases in Iraq. There was no Burger King or Dairy Queen, no gymnasium, no recreation room with a pool table and big-screen television. Meals consisted of field rations, and the Marines worked out using a few makeshift weights in the courtyard. There was just one computer, with an unreliable Internet connection, that the troops could use to send e-mails to family and friends.

Life at Nasser was all about work. Marines who weren't pulling guard duty were sleeping, keeping the base in order, or patrolling with the Iraqis. Every day brought more of the same. To relieve the drudgery, Yale reprised his class-clown role. He'd take the Chiclets gum from ration packs and stick pieces in the place of his two missing front teeth, then flash a smile, just to make his buddies laugh.

In January 2008, Yale's best friend in the battalion, Lance Corporal Curtis Christensen, killed himself on a nearby base. Yale's cheery persona vanished overnight. He cried and seethed, telling his friends that Christensen had been selfish to take his life. And he began to keep to himself.

Then it was time to pack up. The platoon would be leaving Nasser on April 25. The news sent a jolt of excitement through the platoon. It had been a remarkable deployment, especially for Ramadi. None of the Marines at Nasser had been killed or injured. Nobody had been sent home for misbehavior. The Iraqi cops had been trained as planned.

Before they could depart, the old guys had to show the new guys around. Troops call this training period a RIP—relief in place. At an outpost as small as Nasser, defending the perimeter was at the top of the list of priorities. The seasoned platoon decided to begin the process on April 22, the day after the One-Nine guys arrived.

Almost twenty-five years earlier, on the morning of October 23, 1983, a nineteen-ton Mercedes-Benz truck had sped onto the grounds of the Beirut International Airport, toward a four-story building housing a battalion of American Marines. The sentries at the gate previously had been ordered to keep their weapons at "condition four"—no magazines inserted, no rounds in the chamber. By the time one of them managed to get a shot off, it was too late. The truck had crashed into the building's entryway, and the driver detonated a fuel-air bomb equivalent to twenty-one thousand pounds of dynamite. Two hundred forty-one American troops, most of them Marines, were killed.

When Major General John Kelly assumed command of all Marine forces in western Iraq in early 2008, Beirut was not far from his mind. He had lost his best friend in the explosion, and in the years that followed, he had studied all of the mistakes that allowed the bomber to get so close to so many sleeping Marines. As he took stock of the war in Iraq—noting the reduction in violence and the willingness of former insurgents to work with the Marines—he concluded that the Americans were winning. But those gains could easily be rolled back, at least in the minds of his countrymen at home.

"We'll lose some guys in firefights. We'll lose some guys to IEDs," he told his subordinates. "But the thing that will lose us this war is if we have a Beirut-like bombing. That would be a disaster."

As he traveled to big Marine bases and small combat outposts, he always scrutinized what the military calls "force protection." Are there enough barriers? Do the watch towers provide a sufficient view? Does everyone assigned to an entry control point know protocol?

The last question was the most important. Protecting the force from a Beirut-style bomb required that grunts on guard duty be alert, be prepared to fire, and be willing to stand and fight.

As early morning light slanted through the windows, sustained gunfire reverberated through the station. Marines who were awake perked up. The clatter was too loud for someone to be shooting at them. It had to be people on Nasser, shooting out. That was about all anyone's brain could process.

Before the Marines in Nasser's barracks could step out to investigate, they were propelled from their bunks and lifted off their feet, then slammed into the walls and onto the floor, as if they were toy soldiers in a diorama that had been upended. The explosion was so intense that most of the Marines went temporarily deaf. All they could hear was a loud ringing.

"Have we been hit with a fucking nuclear bomb?" one shouted.

Team leader Teague had been knocked through a plywood wall. The Marine next to him had blood coming down his face. Another was spitting blood from his mouth. Teague picked himself up, grabbed his rifle, and climbed up to the roof.

Nothing was as it had looked when he went to bed. The buildings inside Nasser, the brick wall around the station, and the gate had been blown apart. Cinder blocks, chunks of metal, the remnants of sandbags, and shards of glass were scattered across the ground. He glanced toward the entrance, where ECP One had been. All he saw was a giant crater.

The truck had been carrying two thousand pounds of explosives. The force of the blast was so great that the truck's engine block landed fifty yards away, in the bed of an Iraqi police pickup.

Two medics, one each from Haerter's and Yale's units, ran to where the guards would have been standing. They found the men amid the rubble, ripped apart. Haerter was lifeless. Yale was bleeding profusely but still had a pulse. As the medics began to render first aid, one of them shouted, "We need to get him out of here."

Teague tried to get on his radio, but it had been damaged in the explosion, as had every other one at the station. He scrambled to cobble together pieces of two broken radios and then load them with the necessary cryptographic data so he could call the company's headquarters and ask them to send a medevac helicopter.

The medics decided not to wait. They loaded Yale into a Humvee and rode with him to the headquarters, figuring it would be easier to land a helicopter there.

Twenty minutes later, Yale was aboard a helicopter rushing to the main trauma center in western Iraq. The in-flight paramedic tried to keep his blood pressure up, his heart pumping, and his lungs breathing. But his wounds were too grave. Despite shots of epinephrine and shocks from a defibrillator, his heart stopped during the flight.

As they surveyed the devastation, the survivors at Nasser assumed the gunfire they had heard had been their two buddies firing to keep the truck from ramming the gate, but nobody could be sure. There had been no American witnesses to the attack.

General Kelly arrived at Nasser the next morning. He wasn't in the habit of visiting attack sites, but this one had caught his attention: an early morning truck bomb, with reports of gunfire from the ECP, and two dead Marines who had been on guard duty.

It could have been another Beirut, he thought.

Kelly talked to the survivors. Several told him they believed Haerter and Yale had saved all of the Marines inside the security station by staying at their post and shooting at the truck, preventing the driver from entering and forcing him to detonate the bomb outside the gate. Then Kelly summoned his interpreter and went over to talk to the Iraqi policemen. The Marines at Nasser had been too busy cleaning up to question them. One Iraqi said he had been sitting on a chair next to the gate. Although he had run away, he had seen enough to know what happened. The two Marines, he said, gave their lives to keep the truck from barreling into the compound.

"Sir," he told Kelly, "no sane man would have done what those two men did."

He began to cry, confessing to Kelly that he had been an insurgent a few years earlier and had participated in attacks on Americans. Now he was in awe of two of his former adversaries.

"No one would have done that, unless you were a crazy man," he said. "I learned yesterday that Marines are crazy."

Two other Iraqis told Kelly a similar story.

After Kelly departed, one of the Marines in Haerter's squad, Lance Corporal Mario Garcia, recalled that a security camera had been trained on the gate. The computer recording the video had been damaged in the blast, but Garcia fiddled with the machine, eventually connecting the storage disk to a working computer.

He watched the six seconds of video that showed the tanker truck swerving through the concrete barriers. Then he watched it again. He saw the Iraqi cop running away. And once more, his eyes trained on the bottom left of the screen. There was ECP One. He couldn't see who was inside. But he saw puffs of smoke, the telltale sign that those inside were firing their weapons.

"These guys had a set of balls that very few men possess," Garcia said. "They were the ideal Marines. They stood their ground."

When Teague saw the tape a few days later—he had been taken to a hospital after the attack to be treated for a concussion—he was overcome with gratitude. "If they had run, we all would have died," he said.

A week later, just before they were due to fly home, members of both battalions held a memorial service for Haerter and Yale at the headquarters base. Before it began, Rowe, the senior sergeant in Yale's company, gathered his men and told them he had reenlisted in the Corps in honor of Yale.

"A lot of you misjudged him. You didn't think he was a very good Marine," Rowe said. "Well, you had no idea what was really inside him. He gave his life to save all of you."

=★=

Haerter and Yale are among a small fraternity of American troops who have sacrificed their lives for their comrades. They joined Jason Dunham, a Marine who threw himself on a grenade that had been thrown by an insurgent, saving the lives of at least two other Marines. They joined Michael Monsoor, a Navy SEAL, who also leaped on a grenade that was hurled in his direction instead of running away, protecting two of his teammates. And they joined Ross McGinnis, a private first class in the Army who similarly smothered with his body a grenade that had been tossed into his Humvee, saving four other occupants of the vehicle.

What drives a man to give his life to save his comrades from an imminent threat, to decide in just a few seconds to offer the ultimate sacrifice? There are so few who commit altruistic suicide—and even fewer who display such courage and then miraculously survive—that psychologists do not fully understand the range of motivations. Military commanders chalk it up to lessons imparted during training, to esprit de corps, to the ethos of a war fighter. But most troops, when faced with a grenade in their midst, dive in the other direction. Among those who didn't—and lived to tell about it—was Staff Sergeant Leroy Petry, the Army Ranger we wrote about earlier. He regarded his fellow soldiers as family and decided in a split second to risk his life to save theirs. He grabbed the grenade with his right hand and tossed it, and as he did so, it exploded. He lost his hand, but he saved himself and two of his comrades.

What made Haerter and Yale stand and shoot when they could have run? We'll never know for certain. It is difficult to imagine that they thought they could survive the blast of a truck bomb. Perhaps they hoped they could kill the driver before he had a chance to detonate the explosives. They had six seconds, which was more than enough time to understand that either the driver could be forced to detonate outside the gate, almost certainly killing both of them, or they could try to save themselves, the driver would make it inside the station, and everyone in the barracks would die. Six seconds suggests this was not just instinct, not men mindlessly adhering to their military training. They chose to try to save thirty-three fellow Americans and twenty Iraqis.

Dunham, Monsoor, McGinnis, and Petry—four men who lunged at grenades—all received the Medal of Honor, the nation's top decoration for combat gallantry. Although no two service members gave their lives to save more comrades, Haerter and Yale were instead nominated for the Navy Cross. Service crosses are the second-highest award for valor.

Marine officers involved in the decision say they worried a Medal of Honor nomination would have been caught up in years of Pentagon reviews and might even have been rejected because of the lack of American eyewitnesses. The video footage, of course, was key evidence, but not all of the officers who signed off on the Navy Cross were aware of the recording at the time.

It was a mistake not to nominate the two men for the Medal of Honor, said Lieutenant General Richard Mills, then Kelly's deputy commander. "What they did was the epitome of what you expect an American Marine to do. They made a conscious decision to sacrifice themselves. They had to have known the potential—and they stood their ground."

Regardless, the story of April 22, 2008, has entered Marine Corps lore. Young Marines, fresh out of boot camp, are told the story of how two men too young to have had a legal drink before heading to war prevented another Beirut. Veterans hear it too, often from Kelly and Mills.

On November 13, 2010, Kelly stood before a packed hotel ballroom next to the Gateway Arch in St. Louis. He had traveled from

Washington, where he was serving as the commander of all Marine reserve forces, to deliver a lunchtime speech commemorating the Corps' 235th birthday. Four days earlier, his son Marine First Lieutenant Robert Kelly had been killed by a mine in Afghanistan. General Kelly, in his dress blues, his chest lined with two rows of medals, his baldpate reflecting an overhead spotlight, closed his speech not with a eulogy to his son but with the tale of Haerter and Yale.

You can watch the last six seconds of their young lives. Putting myself in their heads, I suppose it took about a second for the two Marines to separately come to the same conclusion about what was going on once the truck came into their view at the far end of the alley. Exactly no time to talk it over, or call the sergeant to ask what they should do. Only enough time to take half an instant and think about what the sergeant told them to do only a few minutes before: "Let no unauthorized personnel or vehicles pass." The two Marines had about five seconds left to live.

It took maybe another two seconds for them to present their weapons, take aim, and open up. By this time the truck was halfway through the barriers and gaining speed the whole time. Here, the recording shows a number of Iraqi police, some of whom had fired their AKs, now scattering like the normal and rational men they were—some running right past the Marines. They had three seconds left to live.

For about two seconds more, the recording shows the Marines' weapons firing nonstop, the truck's windshield exploding into shards of glass as their rounds take it apart and tore into the body of the son-of-a-bitch who is trying to get past them to kill their brothers—American and Iraqi— bedded down in the barracks totally unaware of the fact that their lives at that moment depended entirely on two Marines standing their ground. If they had been aware, they would have known they were safe, because two Marines stood between them and a crazed suicide bomber. The recording shows the truck careening to a stop immediately in front of the two Marines. In all of the instantaneous violence, Yale and Haerter never hesitated. By all reports and by the recording, they never stepped back. They never even started to step aside. They never even shifted their weight. With their feet spread shoulder width apart, they leaned into the danger, firing as fast as they could work their weapons. They had only one second left to live.

The truck explodes. The camera goes blank. Two young men go to their God. Six seconds. Not enough time to think about their families, their country, their flag, or about their lives or their deaths, but more than enough time for two very brave young men to do their duty—into eternity. That is the kind of people who are on watch all over the world tonight—for you.

CHAPTER FIVE

Just Doing My Job

Kyle White awoke to a fusillade of automatic weapons fire so loud that he thought he was having a nightmare.

No way that's real. It's too close.

Then there was a series of even louder blasts. *Rocket-propelled grenades.* His plywood hut shook as if it had been struck by an earthquake.

"Get up, Whitey!" shouted his bunk mate, Specialist Jason Baldwin. "We're being hit." White, twenty years old and also a specialist—the third-lowest rank in the Army—pulled his body armor over his T-shirt, tossed on his helmet, and grabbed his rifle. There was no time to tie his boots. The Taliban, he assumed, had succeeded in getting dangerously close to the perimeter of the Ranch House. That's what he and the rest of his platoon called the tiny cluster of wooden buildings and sandbagged bunkers on a steep hillside in eastern Afghanistan that had been their home for the past four months.

White opened the door, but as soon as he did, a volley of AK-47 rounds hissed by his head. The cracks of the shots, which he expected to hear a half second later—bullets travel faster than the speed of sound—were almost instantaneous.

That can't be right, he thought. And then he realized the Taliban were inside the Ranch House.

Seventy audacious insurgents, some dressed in stolen Afghan army uniforms, others in traditional tunics, had surprised twenty-two American soldiers, some of whom weren't even wearing pants. The Talibs had slipped past the outpost's defenses, snipping the wires leading to the claymore mines protecting the perimeter. They had threatened with execution a contingent of private Afghan guards, hired by the Americans to augment security, if they did not flee. And then, in the gray predawn haze of August 22, 2007, the militants walked into the Ranch House.

When the outpost had been established a year earlier by another platoon of U.S. soldiers, the Taliban had not taken kindly to the arrival of Americans in that mountainous corner of Nuristan province. Attacks on the base occurred almost every week. But when White's platoon arrived, the Talibs had appeared to vanish. Not a single round had been fired into the encampment in four months, and White had sometimes wondered if the Taliban had forgotten about them.

Hardly. Instead of continuing their ineffectual campaign of pinprick attacks, the insurgents had pulled back to stage a massive assault. A Taliban propaganda video released weeks later showed fighters with a detailed, hand-drawn map of the outpost, suggesting that they had been watching the Americans from afar to figure out when and where the base was most vulnerable.

White and Baldwin, who had gone to sleep a few hours earlier after an all-night guard shift, grabbed their M4 carbines to join the fight. As soon as they crawled out of their hut, a wave of gunfire forced them back inside. They tried to exit again and were again forced to pull back. Finally, they decided to run through the line of fire to the outpost's mortar pit. Bullets landed around them, kicking up puffs of dirt, and a rocket-propelled grenade exploded against a nearby tree. But they made it.

Baldwin was a mortarman. But the insurgents were too near to be targeted with mortars, according to all of the Army's regulations. Baldwin's rounds, which had a kill radius of thirty meters, were supposed to be used on enemies at least fifty meters away. Then he saw his platoon medic get shot. His squad leader was pinned down. The insurgents were converging from three sides, and some were only ten meters away. Baldwin cranked the tube to a hair from full vertical—a range that would rain mortars down dangerously close to him—and dropped a round. It killed several insurgents. Then he grabbed a crate of hand grenades and threw them one by one at the attackers.

As Baldwin let fly explosives, White ran to the side of the nearest building, the medical hut, and began trying to pick off insurgents with his rifle, using the wall for cover. He sighted a Talib running through an opening in the trees and pulled the trigger. Two rounds hit the man in the right side of his chest. *I drilled him,* White thought.

A moment later, another soldier came out of the medical hut and offered to take White's place, allowing him to sprint over to the platoon's command post. Despite the mortars, the hand grenades, and the withering return fire from the Americans, the insurgents were still inside the outpost. Several were firing rocket-propelled grenades seized from the Afghan guard bunker.

With the threat so close, White figured he should hurl grenades, too. He asked a fellow soldier to toss him one, but when he reached up to catch it, it slipped through his fingers. The grenade, pin still intact, came to rest a few feet away, in the line of fire. White, in the first firefight of his life, didn't stop to think. He ran to grab it as bullets zinged by.

"That was the stupidest thing I've ever seen," said the soldier who threw it.

My amateur-hour moment, White thought later.

Desperate to turn the tide, his platoon leader, Lieutenant Matthew Ferrara, summoned an A-10 jet, which has a cannon that can unleash forty-two hundred rounds a minute, to strafe the outpost. The Americans were shooting at themselves to save themselves.

The mortars and the air strike helped to turn the tide, as did a courageous run through a hail of fire by Staff Sergeant Erich Phillips to flank the insurgents and assist five wounded soldiers in one of the bunkers. At one point, he charged to within three meters of a Taliban fighter who was shooting.

The surviving Talibs retreated ninety minutes after the attack commenced, heading down the hill to the nearby village of Aranas. Amazingly, no Americans were killed, although eleven of the twenty-two soldiers were wounded.

The assault revealed to White that he was serving with selfless comrades. Sergeant Phillips would later receive a Distinguished Service Cross, the nation's second-highest valor award. Lieutenant Ferrara and Specialist Baldwin would each be given a Silver Star.

The ambush also taught White that the Taliban were tougher than he expected. But so was he.

I rose to the occasion, he thought. *I can do this.*

When Kyle White first gazed on the rugged terrain around the Ranch House, his reaction had nothing to do with war. *This would make for an awesome ride,* he thought.

Growing up near Washington State's Mount Rainier, he spent all of his spare time in high school mountain biking or working in a bicycle shop to earn money for new gear. He wasn't much into school.

Biking made him lean and fit, with powerful leg muscles and a marathoner's stamina. His face could belie his fitness—narrow, deep-set eyes made him appear tired. But when he smiled after a grueling ride, he radiated energy.

When he failed to gain admission to Central Washington University, he decided to pursue the only thing that interested him other than biking: serving in the military. He spoke to a Marine recruiter and then told his dad, Curt, who had served in the Army in the early 1970s. His father let fly a few expletives about the Marines and told White that if he wanted to serve, the Army was the only way to go.

After White finished boot camp and airborne school, the Army assigned him to one of its most storied units: the 173rd Airborne Brigade, based in Vicenza, Italy, about forty-five miles west of Venice. The brigade had fought its initial battles during World War I, it was the first major Army unit to serve in Vietnam, it parachuted into Iraq in 2003, and it went to Afghanistan in 2005.

White joined the brigade in 2006 and was assigned to the First Platoon of Chosen Company, part of the brigade's Second Battalion. He became fast friends with a few other greenhorns in the platoon, all of whom called him Whitey.

Told they would be heading to Iraq the following year, he and his fellow soldiers began training for urban combat on level desert terrain. A few months before they were scheduled to ship out, they received new orders: they would be heading back to Afghanistan to beat back Taliban advances across a swath of the east abutting the border with Pakistan.

"You're going to be on the side of a mountain," he remembered one officer telling him. "Everything is straight up or straight down."

Following the Ranch House attack, the platoon withdrew from the little compound and moved to a larger, more fortified base two miles away. Six weeks later, the elders of Aranas invited the American soldiers for a meeting. Battalion leaders liked the idea, figuring the troops could try to befriend the villagers and identify ways to help them before the long, cold winter arrived. The grunts thought it was a terrible idea. They had clear indications from a Taliban propaganda video that some Aranas residents had abetted the Ranch House attack. Nerves churned White's stomach. It sounded to him like a setup.

Sergeant Jeffery Mersman called his father in Kansas and said he had reservations about the mission, telling him "there was no cover on that goat trail" if they were ambushed. The only element of surprise they would have was their arrival: they planned to leave their base just before midnight, walk for two hours using their night-vision goggles, and reach the village well before sunrise— hours before they were expected.

The early arrival time was small comfort to the soldiers. The platoon had never been scared to go out before, but they were now. They all focused on the date they'd be heading out: November 8. Exactly forty-two years earlier, soldiers from the 173rd conducting an operation on the outskirts of Saigon were ambushed by twelve hundred Vietcong troops. Forty-eight Americans were killed.

The year before White and his buddies had arrived in Afghanistan, the country music duo Big & Rich had released "8th of November," a song about the Vietnam battle that hit the Billboard Hot 100. As members of First Platoon assembled their gear late the evening of their departure, taking extra care in cleaning their rifles, one of them began playing the tune on his computer, loud enough for everyone to hear.

On the 8th of November the angels were crying
As they carried his brothers away
With the fire raining down and the hell all around
There were few men left standing that day.

We're going to wind up like those guys, thought Sergeant James Takes.

Fourteen Americans—White, a dozen other soldiers, and a Marine assigned to train Afghan troops, Sergeant Phillip Bocks—set off for Aranas, accompanied by fifteen Afghan soldiers and two interpreters. As they left the base, one of the sergeants staying behind did something he'd never done before a patrol. Going from soldier to soldier, he shook each man's hand. "Take care," he said. "Be safe."

Despite the premonitions, the platoon made it to the village without incident. They dropped their gear in a schoolhouse that had been built a year earlier with U.S. funds but that they believed served as a Taliban field hospital after major attacks. The plan was for half the soldiers to stand guard while the other half caught a few winks before the meeting with the elders. But nobody could sleep.

When day broke, relief washed over everyone.

Maybe we'll survive this after all, thought Takes.

Aranas perched on the side of a mountain. Residents didn't want to build too close to the valley floor, because the Waygal River floods in the spring with melting snow, so instead they constructed a vertical village of narrow, terraced fields and homes that almost sat on top of each other.

The meeting was supposed to take place mid-morning outside the village mosque. As the designated hour neared, Lieutenant Ferrara, the leader of the American team, asked a few villagers where the elders were. Praying, he was told. An hour later, he inquired again. Still praying, the villagers said.

Finally, at one o'clock, the soldiers left the schoolhouse and walked to the mosque for the meeting. They had expected a dozen mostly gray-bearded residents—talking with Americans wasn't a popular activity in that part of the country, especially among the younger generations—but more than thirty men were gathered, including those in their twenties and thirties.

Maybe they really do want our help, White thought.

Ninety minutes into the meeting, one of the interpreters rushed up to Sergeant Bocks with disturbing intelligence. The interpreter had been listening to a radio scanner that allowed him to pick up nearby walkie-talkie transmissions. Seasoned Taliban fighters knew the Americans were listening, so they often used their radios for boastful taunts and misleading battlefield communication. This chatter was in a language the interpreter had never heard before, suggesting that non-Afghan fighters were nearby. Bocks sidled up to Lieutenant Ferrara.

"We have to go—now!" Bocks said.

Ferrara wrapped up the meeting as quickly as he could without being rude. Twenty minutes later, the soldiers began to walk back to their base. Instead of retracing the path they had taken the night before, they walked along the opposite side of the valley, on a goat-herding trail carved into the side of a mountain. This was a more direct route, but on the largely barren mountain there were precious few trees and shrubs for shade or concealment.

The thirty-one American and Afghan troops moved single file. James Takes took the lead, followed by Specialist Jon Albert, a stocky Iowa farm boy, who carried a machine gun. Eight soldiers followed them. Then came the headquarters element: Ferrara, Bocks, Specialist Kain Schilling, and White, who was the platoon leader's radio operator. Behind them were the interpreters and the Afghan troops.

After twenty-five minutes of hiking, Ferrara ordered the men to stop for a rest. The Afghan soldiers hadn't brought enough water and were winded.

"Come on, man, we've got to go," Takes vented to Albert. The Afghans, he said, "need to step it up."

Five minutes later, Ferrara ordered the column to resume moving. A minute later, a shot rang out. Takes thought one of the tired Afghan soldiers had accidentally discharged his weapon. Then a few more rounds echoed across the valley. Seconds later, recalled Takes, "the whole damn mountain lit up."

The Talibs had picked the perfect spot to ambush the Americans. Not only was the platoon completely exposed, it was blind. Many of the attackers were across the quarter-mile-wide valley, in the shade, with the setting sun at their backs, rendering them almost invisible to the Americans. Another band of insurgents was above the platoon, firing down. The Americans, bathed in orange light, made easy prey.

With bullets smacking into the mountainside on White's left and right, and no way to move up or down, he dropped to his right knee to make himself a smaller target. He pointed his M4 across the valley and unleashed a full clip of ammunition as quickly as he could pull the trigger. He couldn't pick out a target, so he shot in the direction from which he thought the hostile fire was emanating.

KYLE WHITE, TAKING A REST, FIVE MINUTES
BEFORE THE AMBUSH COMMENCED

As he released the empty clip and reached down to pull a full one from his flak vest, a rocket-propelled grenade exploded against the mountain less than a yard away and knocked him out. He awoke facedown on the trail, his skin peppered with shrapnel and rock fragments. He glanced down at his limbs. *Got them.* He put his hand to his face. It was covered in blood, but he couldn't feel anything missing. *Keep fighting.*

No sooner had that thought crossed his mind than he heard Kain Schilling, a skinny Iowan with tattoos along his left arm who had been directly in front of him before the ambush, scream in pain. Schilling had been shot in his right shoulder, and White saw him scurry toward a tree growing below the trail whose sparse canopy offered the only hope of concealment.

White, still carrying his backpack radio, ran toward Schilling. Rounds snapped by, but he knew his buddy needed help applying a tourniquet to stanch the bleeding. Once he had reached the tree and aided Schilling, White poked his rifle through the canopy and resumed firing.

A moment later, he noticed an acrid smell. He and Schilling began to choke.

Holy shit, he thought. *Are they using chemical weapons on us?*

Then Schilling said, "Your radio is on fire." A bullet had ignited the lithium battery. The sight reminded White that he needed to call the base to report the ambush and summon help. He tried to use Schilling's radio, but it, too, was dead. So he resumed shooting.

"Bocks has been hit," Schilling shouted at him a few seconds later.

Bocks had been hit twice, in the right thigh and the left shoulder. He was sitting upright about ten yards away, weapon slung across his chest. Blood oozed from his mouth.

"Get to me," White yelled at him. "Use all of your strength to get to me."

Bocks tried to scoot toward White and Schilling, but he was too hurt to move. A Taliban shooting gallery separated them. The insurgents were using not just AK-47 rifles but belt-fed machine guns and rocket-propelled grenades. And it seemed as if dozens of insurgents were firing from multiple directions.

White had met Bocks a few days earlier. Wearing a desert camouflage uniform, Bocks was the odd American out, the sole Marine among a platoon of soldiers. While most of his buddies were heading to Iraq, he had volunteered for the arduous mission of training Afghan troops. He and White didn't share the bond forged between comrades who had endured boot camp together, passed nights in Vicenza bars, and faced down the earlier attack on the Ranch House. But Bocks was a fellow warrior.

I'm gonna die up here, thought White. *I might as well try to help my buddies until I get shot up.*

He ran to Bocks. As he did, the volume of fire increased. The Talibs were concentrating their shots on the men still standing, not the downed ones. Some of the rounds were so close White could feel them whoosh by.

He began to pull Bocks by a canvas strap fastened to the back of his flak vest. But he worried that the increase in fire put Bocks in greater danger. "I dragged him a few feet and then made the decision to run back to Kain to draw their attention, to keep their focus on me," White recalled. "I wasn't worrying about me getting hit, but I knew Bocks couldn't sustain another gunshot wound. So I did that. I ran back to Kain, and they followed me with their fire. And then when I got behind that concealment of the tree, they would lose focus or just wait. So I'd wait just a couple seconds and then repeat the movement. I did that like three or four times."

When White was finally able to drag Bocks behind the tree, he tied a tourniquet around Bocks's right thigh, then pulled off the Marine's body armor to treat the shoulder wound. The bullet's entrance was no wider than a pinkie finger, but it had ricocheted around inside his chest. The exit wound, below Bocks's rib cage, was grim.

"I don't think I'm going to make it through this one," Bocks gasped.

"You're gonna be fine," White told him. "We'll get you out of here soon."

A minute later, Bocks was dead.

White turned to tell Schilling. At that instant, a bullet flew through the canopy and struck Schilling in the left knee. Time for another tourniquet. But White had used his on Bocks. Desperate to stop the bleeding, White took off his belt.

"This is going to hurt," he warned Schilling.

"I don't care," Schilling replied. "Just do it."

So White placed his foot on Schilling's thigh and pulled the belt as hard as he could. With Schilling stabilized, White looked up the trail for any sign of his comrades. It was then he saw Lieutenant Ferrara's helmet and backpack.

Once again, White left the tree canopy and braved the field of fire. This time, however, he crawled. When he reached Ferrara, he found him dead. His radio had been destroyed.

An emergency room's worth of adrenaline was still coursing through White's veins, but his fatalistic fearlessness was giving way to dejection. Two comrades were dead. Everyone's radio was busted. White crawled back to the tree.

When he returned to Schilling, White wondered if Bocks's radio was working. It was. White lifted the handheld microphone. As he brought it to his face, a Talib bullet bored a hole through the device.

"You've got to be kidding me," he said to Schilling.

White figured a work-around. He disconnected the handset and brought the radio to his mouth like an old-fashioned walkie-talkie. He announced himself by his call sign.

"This is Charlie One Six Romeo."

The sound of his voice sent a wave of relief through the operations center on the platoon's base. They knew about the ambush. They could hear the gunfire and explosions reverberating through the valley.

White reported that he and Schilling were alive, that Ferrara and Bocks were dead. The base asked about the ten soldiers in the front of the column. White had no idea.

When the valley erupted in gunfire, James Takes and Jon Albert, the first two soldiers in the line, looked for something, anything, to shield them from the incoming bullets. All they could find was a two-foot-wide rock, not enough cover for one man, let alone two. But they had nothing else.

Both soldiers knelt behind it and began firing. As they did, Takes noticed some of the incoming rounds were landing close to his right side.

"Slot over," he said to Albert. "I'm getting shot here."

"Fuck you," Albert replied. "I'm getting shot *here*."

As rocket-propelled grenades flew their way, exploding within a few yards, Takes figured there was only one way they would survive: *We've got to get off this mountain.*

And that meant heading straight down the cliff.

"We've got to go," he shouted to Albert. "They've got us pinned down."

As four soldiers behind them rushed forward, Takes eyed an outcropping below that appeared to provide cover. But to reach it, they would have to slide and tumble down a nearly sheer rock face.

"Go!" he screamed. "I'll cover you."

After the others had jumped, Takes followed. As he did, a bullet struck his right arm.

The outcropping turned out to provide miserable concealment, so the soldiers kept rolling down the mountain, their helmets and backs and knees banging against rocks. They finally reached a ledge, which they began to cross so they could keep heading down, only to be spotted by the insurgents. Fire rained down again.

"Fuck," Takes yelled. "We've got to move."

As they resumed scrambling down, Albert was hit in the knee. He was unable to walk, so Takes held him by his flak vest. He grabbed a tuft of grass with his other hand to keep from falling.

"Just let go," Albert implored.

Takes was reminded of the scene in the movie *Titanic* when the two lovers are in the ocean clinging to a piece of wood that can only support one.

"I'll never let go," he vowed to his friend.

But the grass gave way, and they both fell farther.

Takes looked for another place to hunker down. He spotted a crack in another outcropping large enough to shield a man. He hauled Albert over, ribbing him along the way. "God, you're so fat," he said, before tying a tourniquet around his leg. As he got up to resume firing, Takes was shot in the muscle of his other arm.

Fuck. Could this day get any worse?

They eventually found a less steep path to the base of the valley, where they came upon four comrades near the bank of the Waygal River. One of them, Specialist Sean Langevin, was dead. Another was too injured to move. Two others helped Takes treat the wounded and keep a lookout for any Talibs who might try to storm their position.

Then Takes got on the radio. He called for a medical evacuation helicopter: Albert and Private First Class Justin Kalenits, whose pelvis had been shattered, he said, were "urgent surgical" priority cases. Takes was told there was too much hostile fire to send in the choppers. So he began communicating with mortarmen at the base to direct high-explosive rounds at the insurgents.

He had no idea what had happened to anyone else in the platoon. The lieutenant? Their medic? The Marine?

Then he caught the steady voice of Charlie One Six Romeo on the radio.

Kyle's alive.

As the sun set behind the mountain on which most of the insurgents had perched, the firing ebbed. The Talibs, who lacked night-vision goggles, couldn't spot their prey in the nearly moonless night. Although White and Takes never said so over the radio, they shared the same concern: Might the lull in shooting mean that the Taliban were trying to sneak up and besiege them from close range?

Had the 173rd Airborne soldiers been in Iraq instead of Afghanistan, help from the sky would have arrived less than fifteen minutes into the ambush, perhaps in the form of an AH-64 Apache attack helicopter, which carries a 30-millimeter chain gun and sixteen Hellfire missiles; or a supersonic F-16 fighter with five-hundred-pound satellite-guided bombs; or an AC-130 Spectre gunship, equipped with a cannon that spits out four-inch-wide rounds. But in 2007, the Afghanistan campaign was the Pentagon's "economy of force" war. Most of the military's aircraft were in Iraq to support the troop surge there. Overextended air support crews in Afghanistan did not always show up with the haste of a Domino's Pizza delivery.

Two Apaches had hovered over the platoon as it left Aranas, but those birds had pulled away before the ambush, summoned to a different valley because another contingent of 173rd soldiers had gotten into a gunfight. By the time White got on the radio to request help, the only available aircraft was a B-1 bomber, which arrived ninety minutes into the attack. It dropped three separate one-thousand-pound bombs on the insurgents. Other aircraft arrived soon after, but their crews needed to assess the ongoing threat before medical helicopters could enter the valley.

On the trail and in the valley, White and Takes sought to keep themselves and their wounded comrades alive. As the sun vanished and the temperature dipped to just above freezing, White bundled Schilling in a poncho to keep him warm.

"Where are they?" Schilling asked about the medevac choppers.

"They're on the way," White replied, patting Schilling's head, as he scanned the trail in both directions.

Schilling repeated the question every few minutes. White kept offering the same answer. The truth was that he didn't know. The helicopters should have arrived by then. He had described Schilling as "urgent surgical."

And then he heard the crunch-crunch of approaching footsteps on the trail.

Here comes the next attack, he thought.

White flipped the safety on his M4 to semiautomatic and raised it to fire. Then he heard the voice of Bocks's interpreter.

"Here comes the ANA," the interpreter said, using the acronym for the Afghan National Army. Several of the Afghan soldiers who had been at the end of the column came into view.

Using the interpreter, White directed them to guard both sides of the trail. His head was throbbing from the successive grenade explosions, and he began to worry that he would pass out, leaving Schilling alone with the Afghans.

When he finally heard the clatter of an approaching helicopter and a medic dropped down in a harness, White sent Schilling up first, then two wounded Afghan soldiers, and then a bundle of broken radios and other gear he didn't want to fall into Taliban hands. Only then did he get lifted out.

As the UH-60 Black Hawk climbed over the ridge and headed to the nearest base with a field hospital, White stared out the window.

I think I made it.

A second helicopter pulled out the soldiers at the bottom of the valley. Takes, like White, sent everyone else up first, including Sean Langevin's lifeless body. When Takes eventually made it aboard, he had one request of the flight crew: "Let's get the fuck out of here."

It would take fifteen more hours for fellow soldiers from the 173rd, working with Air Force Special Operations rescue personnel, to locate the bodies of the three other platoon members who had not been discovered by White or Takes. Two had been killed on the trail between White and Takes. Another had attempted to slide down the mountainside but never made it.

Soon after White and Takes arrived at the main U.S. trauma center in eastern Afghanistan, they learned the full list of who hadn't come back alive:

Jeffery Mersman, the sergeant from Kansas who had called his father the night before to share his worries about the mission. He had accumulated enough credits in high school that he was able to leave for boot camp halfway through his senior year, when he was just seventeen. He had deployed to Iraq three times before coming to Afghanistan with the 173rd.

Joseph Lancour, a specialist from Michigan who manned one of the platoon's machine guns. He was a stick—five foot nine and 120 pounds at boot camp—who had been a punter and placekicker on his high school football team. He had enlisted in 2006 and joined the platoon at the same time White had.

Lester Roque, the platoon medic, who signed up for the Army as soon as he emigrated from the Philippines in 2004. He was on his second deployment in Afghanistan.

Phil Bocks, the Marine adviser, who had overcome problems with depression and attention-deficit disorder. A visit with a church youth group to the Marine Corps Recruit Depot on Parris Island, South Carolina, hooked the Michigan native on the Corps.

Matt Ferrara, a 2005 West Point graduate who ran cross-country and spoke Mandarin Chinese. He had grown up in Torrance, California, one of four brothers, all of whom joined the military. He wrote home to ask his parents to send socks and baby wipes for the platoon—showers were a rare treat—not to regale them with war stories. His parents would only learn about the Ranch House attack, and his receipt of a Silver Star, after his death.

And Sean Langevin of Walnut Creek, California. He was Whitey's best friend and a fellow adventure seeker. Langevin had brought his wife, Jessica, to Vicenza, where they lived in a two-bedroom apartment outside the U.S. base. White and Jon Albert would come over almost every weekend to eat and play beer pong and then carouse through the town. They were such frequent visitors that Jessica bought them their own air mattresses. When they were in Afghanistan, Sean tried to phone Jessica, whom he had met while they were working in the same pizza parlor, every day.

White was released from the hospital after three days. The doctors had kept him to observe his recovery from the multiple concussions he sustained on the trail. Then he received dispensation from his commanders to make a brief trip back to the United States to attend the funerals for Lancour and Langevin.

Angry and grief stricken, he kept to himself, smoking out on the sidewalk, refusing to make small talk with other mourners, except for Jessica, who was six months pregnant. Sitting in her parents' home, he told her that he and Sean had agreed, back at the Ranch House, that if anything happened to either one of them, they would care for each other's family. "I'll be there for both of you," he said. "Whatever you need."

He returned to Afghanistan two weeks later. When he arrived at his battalion's headquarters, the commander of Chosen Company, Captain Matthew Myer, summoned him for a conversation.

What you did, Myer told White, "was a very big deal." Myer said his boss, Lieutenant Colonel William Ostlund, would be nominating him for the Medal of Honor. White's actions on the trail, Ostlund concluded, had been selfless and smart. He had saved Schilling, and he had risked his life multiple times to pull Bocks to safety. He had helped to direct mortar fire against the insurgents, organize the Afghan soldiers, and keep sensitive gear from being seized by the enemy. The voice of Charlie One Six Romeo on the radio had provided Ostlund and his staff with "situational awareness when we were absolutely blind and confused." White, he said, had "won the day when the day was all but lost."

To White, a Medal of Honor seemed unnecessary, irrelevant even. He was doing his job as a soldier up there on the trail. If the roles had been reversed and he had been severely injured, he believed any of his comrades would have done what he had.

"I just did the best I could," he said. "It doesn't seem to me that I did all that much."

A few days after he returned from the United States, he went back out on patrol. So did Takes, whom Ostlund nominated for a Distinguished Service Cross. They conducted missions for seven more months, until it was time to return to Italy.

"Those guys were my family," White said. "All I wanted to do was to be back with them."

As the months passed, though, he realized that he had left part of himself on the trail that November afternoon. He had entered the Army planning on a twenty-year career, but he didn't think that his head was fully back in the game. He worried that it would be wrong to continue serving if he was not operating at 100 percent. When his enlistment was up, he left the Army.

He moved to Charlotte to open a power-tool business with Takes. When that failed to succeed as White had hoped, he focused on his course work at the University of North Carolina at Charlotte. He resolved not to take easy classes with his GI Bill funds. He majored in business administration, which involved math—his worst subject in high school. To his surprise, his first semester he earned straight A's.

"College was a breeze," he said. "There was always a solution. If you have a problem, you can look in a book and find the answer. Other things in life aren't that easy—especially in war."

Outside the classroom was where he met challenges. He struggled with post-traumatic stress, experiencing flashbacks to the ambush and bouts of anger. He refused to take antidepressants and sleeping pills, preferring instead to sweat out his demons in the gym.

The easiest part of the event to push to the recesses of his brain was the Medal of Honor submission, which was winding its way through the Pentagon bureaucracy. Most Medal of Honor nominations die on the desks of Pentagon brass because they fail to pass the stringent requirements for incontrovertible evidence that a service member engaged in an act of valor with the near certainty that he or she would perish.

White graduated from college in 2013. The following January, he was hired as an analyst in the Charlotte office of the Royal Bank of Canada. His new colleagues knew he had been in the Army, but none of them had any idea what he had done in Afghanistan on November 9, 2007.

About two weeks after he started the job, White received a cryptic phone call from the Pentagon. A senior military official, he was told, would call him on February 10.

His mobile phone rang at the appointed hour.

"Please hold for the President of the United States," he was instructed.

President Obama informed White that he would be receiving the Medal of Honor. He spoke of White's bravery, his selflessness, his leadership.

"I was just doing my job, Mr. President," White responded.

Three months later, White stood in the East Room of the White House next to the thirteen-star Medal of Honor flag, his hands clasped behind his back, his face as solemn as it was during his first meeting with a drill sergeant, as Obama recounted his actions on the trail to members of White's family, his girlfriend, fellow soldiers from Chosen Company, and the relatives of several of those who died that day.

The president told the crowd that White wears a stainless-steel bracelet around his wrist etched with the names of his six comrades who died on the mountainside. Then he quoted White: "Their sacrifice motivates me to be the best I can be. Everything I do in my life is done to make them proud."

Obama looked at White. "You make us proud," he said, "and you motivate all of us to be the best we can be as Americans."

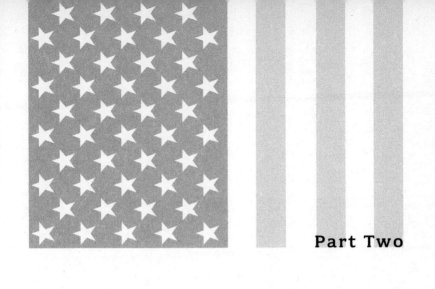

Part Two

CHAPTER SIX

You're All Going to College

D avid Oclander bounded through a Roman-columned entrance-
way and into the oldest public education building in Chicago,
now home to a college-prep charter school. At nine thirty in the
morning, he stood by the door of his classroom, greeting each of
his thirty-four pupils. Ahead was one final sophomore English
lesson—and then summer. This class was a chance for the students
to celebrate completing another year of school in a city where the
dropout rate averages 40 percent, and a chance for Mr. O. to celebrate completing his second year of teaching.

Oclander looked each kid in the eye as he or she passed.

"Hey, great essay."

Another student got a fist bump.

"Much improvement."

"You got a paper for me?" he asked another.

The students, dressed in polo shirts and khakis, sat in clusters of
four desks, as if dining at tables in a restaurant. After the bell rang,
Oclander walked in and told them to take three deep breaths. "As
you breathe out, I want you to push out the thoughts of summer. I
want you present and focused right now."

Two-thirds of the class was Hispanic, the rest African American. Almost all of the students qualified for federally funded
breakfasts and lunches. They hailed from Chicago's toughest neigh-

DAVID OCLANDER

borhoods, where drugs were hawked on the corners and gunfire was heard nightly. They hoped this aging West Side building, where a young Walt Disney walked the halls almost a century earlier and which now stands in the shadow of the United Center sports arena, would be their ticket out. The school, Chicago Bulls College Prep, had been endowed by the charitable arm of the city's eponymous professional basketball team. And so the kids trekked here every morning, some traveling as much as an hour on buses and trains.

The previous week, Oclander had invited an Ethiopian refugee to share with the class his remarkable journey to the ivy-strewn campus of Harvard. Of all the advice the young man imparted, Oclander asked his students, "What was the most meaningful for you?"

"Don't study what you know," one boy said.

Oclander followed up with a reference to a popular exercise program. "Who loves doing CrossFit?"

Hands shot up.

"Not all of you like the same exercises. Some of you prefer to run. Some of you like to lift weights." He quoted one of the founders of CrossFit: "He'd tell you, 'Those things you don't like to do— go straight at them.'"

He strode over to a student slouching in his seat and glared. When a girl started to stumble through an answer to a question he posed, he cut her off. "No 'ums.' No 'likes.'"

She rolled her eyes.

"My class, my rules," he said.

Another student said he thought the refugee would be taller.

"Stature doesn't mean much," Oclander replied. He pointed at his head. "It's what you carry in here."

Then he passed out the results of a recently administered standardized test.

"Felipe, you're on the way. It's clear you're putting in the effort," he said to one young man.

"Hey, you've got the potential," he said to another, "but you have to realize it."

Some of the students took a look at their numbers and turned glum. A girl named Kayla said that she was thinking of dropping out. Oclander walked over and squatted down next to her so they were at eye level.

"I've failed so many times I've stopped counting," he said. "Failing doesn't define you. I failed classes in college. There were times I failed in my previous profession. If you define yourself by a snapshot in time, you are shortchanging yourself. You're all going to college. You all have the potential."

Kayla remained unconvinced. "School's not for me. I don't want to work my butt off if it doesn't make me happy."

Instead of debating her, he let other students chime in.

"It's just one test," a boy across the room said to her. "It's not that big of a deal."

Another cited Martin Luther King Jr. "We have a moral responsibility to be intelligent."

Then came the year's final writing exercise. Oclander handed out sheets of bright green paper and told the students to write a letter to themselves that they would read the following school year, before they took the ACT college-entrance test.

"Talk about the voices you're going to silence and the voices you're going to listen to," he instructed.

Out of Oclander's earshot, one student whispered to another, "I'm gonna listen to him."

Four years earlier, Oclander had delivered a similar rah-rah talk to soldiers in the badlands of Afghanistan, where he commanded a battalion task force of a thousand paratroopers. They were heading to the outskirts of Kandahar, the second-largest city in the country, where they would be building and manning checkpoints on every road heading into the urban center. It was a dangerous assignment that would leave them exposed to Taliban attacks, but it was an important component of a new U.S. strategy to beat back the insurgency. Keeping his troops focused and confident, and pushing them to learn and stay fit, improved their odds of returning home alive.

An Indiana-raised son of an Argentine immigrant, Oclander had spent his adult life defending his nation. Though he was a talented soccer player, he turned aside recruiting pitches from several universities to enroll in the U.S. Military Academy at West Point. He spent most of the next two decades at the Eighty-Second Airborne Division, rising through the officer ranks. He deployed twice to Iraq and once to Afghanistan. When he returned, he took an assignment planning future military missions on the Pentagon's Joint Staff.

He had long believed the greatest threat to the United States was from overseas. When he had entered college in 1986, everyone had an eye on the Soviet Union. Then came the chaotic postcommunist world. In the decade after the September 11 attacks, al-Qaeda and its extremist allies assumed the mantle.

Oclander's desk in the basement of the Pentagon had three computers. Two were connected to an internal Defense Department network, allowing him to access top secret information. The other, which was linked to the public Internet, he used to keep abreast of world news. The classified network usually provided the more compelling reading, but one day in August 2011 a news headline from Chicago caught his eye: "Boy, 13, Dead from Gunshot on Basketball Court." A week later, he read a story about another child in Chicago who had also been shot to death.

His interest piqued, Oclander began to track homicides in Chicago from his Pentagon office. He compared the tallies of attacks on U.S. troops in Afghanistan that he received through his classified computer with the violent deaths in America's third-largest city. When a news report making that same comparison came out the following year, he already knew what the headline announced: "Chicago Homicides Outnumber U.S. Troop Killings in Afghanistan."

All the foreign dangers he had been studying and the war plans he had helped to design seemed far less significant than what was happening in Chicago. *The greatest threat to our country is no longer overseas, it's within our borders,* he thought to himself. *If we don't get this right, America will no longer be the world's greatest nation.*

Not long after, a member of the men's group at Oclander's church posed a question during a Wednesday morning Bible study. "Are you a fan or a follower of Christ?" Those words knocked around Oclander's head as he thought about the violence in Chicago. He wondered what he, a career soldier, could do. His mind went back to Afghanistan, to the arduous year he had spent in the provinces of Zabul and Kandahar. Ninety percent of the men who lived there were illiterate—and so were 99 percent of the women—making them easy prey for Taliban recruiters. During his deployment, Oclander had grown convinced that education was a prerequisite for long-term stability there. He figured the same held true for America.

Could he trade the Army for a school in a rough-and-tumble neighborhood? He had no formal training in education. He had been in uniform for twenty-two years, much of it in one of the Army's most prestigious divisions. He was a lieutenant colonel with a comfortable military life, and he could leverage his current position into a cushy job with a defense contractor or a private security firm. After all, he had a wife and three children to support. His family was encouraging, but when he told his Pentagon colleagues what he was thinking about doing, they looked at him as if he were crazy. If he really wanted to help, one friend said, he should stay in government or else make lots of money in the corporate world and give it to schools.

Oclander talked to friends in the State Department, the CIA, and the private sector about the jobs open to him. Nothing felt as important as education. If he was going to leave the Army, he didn't want to kick up his heels. He needed to keep serving.

He ruminated and prayed, growing ever surer that he needed to work in a school with at-risk youth. He believed that his years in uniform, his leadership experience, his commitment to fitness, and his experience in mentoring young soldiers, many of them just a year or two out of high school, gave him a special set of skills for working in a classroom.

When Oclander sent out his résumé to some of the country's largest charter school networks and public school systems, he assumed superintendents would be keen to hire him. He heard back from most of them. *Your background is great,* he was told, *but do*

*you have a teaching credential? Do you have classroom experi-
ence?* When he said no, the universal response was "Thanks, but
no thanks."

Unwilling to give up, Oclander tapped West Point's active alumni
network and connected with a fellow academy graduate in Chicago
who ran a mentoring program that introduced middle schoolers to
various professional careers. From him, Oclander learned that Illinois allows charter schools to hire teachers without credentials. The
man urged Oclander to concentrate his search in Chicago and start
by contacting the Noble Network of Charter Schools. When Oclander got in touch with Noble's chief executive, Michael Milkie, he
was invited for an interview.

"I don't have credentials. I don't have classroom experience,"
Oclander told Milkie at the outset. "If that's a deal killer, let me
know and I won't waste your time."

"I hire talent," Milkie said. "I don't hire credentials."

Three months later, dressed in a crisp shirt and a tightly knot-
ted tie, Oclander stood before a room of high school freshmen at a
Noble campus on Chicago's crime-ridden West Side to teach a class
about leadership. He began by talking about the personal failure he
felt when soldiers under his command were killed.

"What we do with our failures makes us the person that we
are," he said. "When we fail, we have two choices: we can quit, and
that becomes a habit, or we can learn and grow from those failures.
If you choose to grow, you can become a great leader."

When Oclander wasn't busy with his own classes, he sometimes
helped another veteran turned teacher at the school, an Illinois
Army National Guard major named Mark Hamstra, to lead a class
that combined CrossFit workouts and history lessons about the
war in Afghanistan. Hamstra, who had served in Afghanistan for

a year, called it Warrior Fit. In one lesson, Oclander and Hamstra described the military's counterinsurgency strategy to the students, explaining to them how the troops switched from solely attacking insurgents to protecting the civilian population as well, in an attempt to deny the Taliban vital local support. The two veterans handed out to the students excerpts from the military's counterinsurgency field manual.

One student said the description of insurgents in Afghanistan sounded no different from how gangs operated in his neighborhood. "How can we apply some of this stuff?" the student asked.

Oclander and Hamstra grinned. They assigned their pupils to develop a plan to adapt the military's counterinsurgency strategy to their streets. What would happen, Hamstra asked, if the Chicago police spent more time winning the confidence of people in the students' neighborhoods?

The students analyzed their communities the same way Army officers did the villages in Iraq and Afghanistan, identifying ethnic and religious composition, levels of unemployment, and prevalence of gang activity. "I will use the COIN [counterinsurgency] philosophy of clear, hold, build to help change West Englewood into a productive neighborhood," one wrote, concluding that more police had to be deployed along two main streets and that residents needed to establish their own neighborhood watch group. "This process will take time, but it will clear the area of any hostile environment."

To Oclander, discussions about counterinsurgency strategy were more than academic. Soon after moving to the city, he started going for walks with his pastor in one of the roughest West Side communities on Saturday nights. They went not to proselytize but to listen to drug dealers, gangbangers, and people just trying to survive. They saw plenty of police, almost always sitting in their squad cars. Oclander told his pastor he had ordered his troops to conduct as many foot patrols as possible in Afghan villages: "You don't dominate anything from inside your vehicle except the space inside your vehicle."

After so many years at war, he wanted to describe his experience in fighting insurgents with the police department. He shared his field assessment with other Iraq and Afghanistan veterans in Chicago, and eventually a group of them paid a visit to the police department's command center. The cops were polite, but they weren't about to turn over policing strategy to a bunch of former soldiers.

Oclander ran into similar skepticism at school. Noble's chief executive had hired him to be a principal in training. The plan was that Oclander would spend three years teaching and learning how the schools operated. Then he'd get his own school. That didn't sit well with some fellow teachers. One told him that he needed "to go through the trenches," an irony that wasn't lost on Oclander. Another complained to Milkie that he had "no idea what you were thinking" when he hired Oclander. "It's been an uphill battle," Oclander said. "But I'm not giving up."

Whenever he got the opportunity, Oclander exhorted fellow veterans to embrace teaching. Among those who heard his pitch was Michael Gaal, an Air Force colonel whom Oclander had befriended a dozen years earlier, when they were classmates at the Marine Corps Command and Staff College.

As he was preparing to end a quarter-century Air Force career, Gaal attended a job fair for graduates of military academies, where he met with recruiters from defense contractors and Fortune 500 corporations. They were keen to talk to him. He had served as the vice-commander of an air wing, and he possessed potentially lucrative knowledge of the regulations governing the sales of American-built aircraft to foreign nations. But the interest wasn't mutual.

Gaal, whose most enjoyable moments in the Air Force had involved training pilots, didn't want a nameplate on the door of a corporate office, even if it would yield a larger paycheck than he had ever seen in the military. Instead, he was mulling becoming a high school math or physics teacher.

He had asked himself a few months earlier, What am I good at? *I'm good at leading people and solving difficult problems.*

He thought about teaching.

This is my difficult problem.

As he was leaving the job fair, Gaal spotted a booth of Teach for America representatives. When he walked over and expressed his interest, he wound up talking to Grant Besser, a senior vice president at the organization, which enlists high-achieving recent college graduates and mid-career professionals to teach in low-income schools. "You remind me a lot of a guy I know in the Army who just made this transition," Besser said.

Privately, Gaal was amused. The Army has half a million soldiers, and he only knew a few of them.

"His name is David Oclander," Besser said. "Any chance you know him?"

Gaal laughed out loud. He told Besser that he and Oclander had met each other twelve years earlier, when they bonded as two non-Marines in a school full of Leathernecks. Gaal, who thought Oclander was the smartest guy he had ever met, told Besser that he wouldn't have bothered to entertain a career in teaching if not for Oclander. "He reaffirmed to me there is a need, a desire, a space for veterans in the classroom," Gaal said.

Gaal wanted to work in a low-performing urban school district, which would befit his military ethos, not in a cushy suburb. "We're trained to run toward the sound of gunfire and chaos," he said. "Why would anyone want to go into the education sector and not take on a big challenge?"

Besser suggested that Gaal, with his leadership experience, consider becoming a school administrator. Gaal was intrigued. But, he wondered, why would any school take a chance on a veteran who had not even spent a day teaching outside the military, especially given the obstacles that Oclander had encountered and described for Gaal? Besser promised to pass along Gaal's résumé to an organization that could help.

A few months later, Gaal was selected for the prestigious Broad Superintendents Academy. Funded by the philanthropist and entrepreneur Eli Broad, the academy trains ten to fifteen executives a year from noneducation fields to become leaders of public and charter school systems.

Halfway through the eighteen-month program, Gaal applied for jobs with some of the nation's most troubled school systems: in Washington, D.C.; Los Angeles; Charlotte; Dallas; Detroit; and Camden, New Jersey. In June 2014, he accepted an offer to become the chief operating officer of the Education Achievement Authority of Michigan, which runs fifteen of Detroit's lowest-performing schools. It was the sort of high-stress job that many educators might view as thankless. Gaal was thrilled.

As he set out for his new job, he sent Oclander a note of thanks.

"Nobody ever wants to get on a roller coaster, but it's easier if your friend gets on before you," Gaal said. "He showed me it could be done."

It didn't take long for students to learn that Mr. O. wasn't like their other teachers. He was a decade or two older, for one thing. And though he didn't make a big deal of it with his students, everyone knew he had been a lieutenant colonel in the Army and had been to war three times.

A few months after Oclander began teaching, Dennis Martir, a junior, figured he'd show up the old soldier. Martir, a Puerto Rican who lacked a ripple of fat on his muscled frame, challenged the new teacher to a push-up contest: Who could do more of them in a minute? Oclander, whose temples have grayed, seemed like an easy mark. But he accepted. The competitor in him couldn't resist a fitness throwdown.

Students around them counted. Martir pumped out forty. Oclander hit sixty.

A few days later, Oclander pulled Martir aside to ask if he had ever thought about applying to a service academy. Martir said he was thinking of enlisting in the Army to become a rank-and-file soldier if he couldn't land a college scholarship. His mother and stepfather worked long hours but barely scraped by. Like almost all of his classmates, if Martir wanted to continue his education, he needed financial assistance.

Oclander explained that the academies provide a four-year college education for free, but they do require a five-year commitment to the armed forces upon graduation. "It sounds like the perfect combination for you," he said, urging Martir to apply for a week-long summer program at West Point that would offer a taste of military academy life, complete with reveille at three o'clock in the morning, classroom sessions, and three-mile runs through the rolling hills along the Hudson River.

Martir went and loved it. The atmosphere of camaraderie at West Point couldn't have been more different from his childhood in Chicago's Hermosa district, where he had learned to be wary of others, and even the environment at his high school, where he was encouraged to work independently in some classes to improve his test scores. "We bonded with each other within the week," he said of his group of aspiring cadets.

They came from across the nation, across the class spectrum, across racial lines. But few others had navigated a path as remarkable as Martir's. In Chicago, Martir's house was located on the fault line between two rival gangs, the Cobras and the Eagles. When he was nine, he watched through his bedroom window as one man shot another on the street below. The gunman spotted young Dennis—a potential witness—and shot at him. The bullet missed his head by inches.

From that day on, his mother, Yolanda, kept him at home when he wasn't at school. There would be no playing basketball on the neighborhood courts or biking through the streets for him and no goofing off at home, either. After watching him attend eight grades of Chicago public schools without being assigned enough work to require his carrying a book bag, his stepfather enrolled him in a Noble charter.

"It was a rough transition," Martir said, but it provided him with a shot at getting out of Hermosa.

When he began his senior year in 2013, Oclander helped him navigate West Point's application process, which requires candidates to be nominated by a member of Congress. Martir's test scores were on the bubble for an academy, but the young man figured that even if he didn't make it, his stepfather would be proud of his perseverance.

That January, Martir's stepfather was killed in a car accident. Two days later, Martir received word that he had been admitted to the academy.

In March, Oclander took Dennis and Yolanda to an annual celebration of West Point's founding, hosted by Chicago-area alumni at a posh country club in the suburbs. As they chatted at the event, Yolanda told Oclander that Dennis's biological father had been one of the city's largest drug dealers and that he had been in prison for much of Dennis's youth. She wanted to know if that would jeopardize her son's ability to get a security clearance. Oclander assured her it wouldn't.

Learning about Martir's father confirmed for Oclander that West Point was the right school for Dennis. The kid was a fighter and a survivor. He had his own moral compass. And his life experience in urban Chicago would bring a fresh perspective to a tradition-bound institution dominated for years by white men raised in rural America. "He knows more about overcoming obstacles than most other kids his age," Oclander said.

Martir had picked up some of that skill on the streets and at home. But it was Oclander, he said, who taught him more than anyone else how to smash through barriers to achieve a goal that he hadn't even known existed twenty months earlier.

"He has made the impossible possible for me," Martir said a few days before his high school graduation.

As the two lunched at a Brazilian restaurant next to Chicago Bulls College Prep, Martir told Oclander he was inspired by his career in uniform as much as he was by what Oclander had to say. "What you did by serving our country was very, very honorable," Martir said. "I want to do the same thing."

He stared at Oclander.

"And when I'm done with being a soldier, I want to be like you. I want to find a way to keep serving my country."

CHAPTER SEVEN

Team Rubicon

On April 27, 2014, Jeff Hunter had spent his entire workday at Fred's Super Dollar, in Vilonia, Arkansas, racked by apprehension. The weather forecast called for severe springtime storms, and there was nothing he disliked more than thunder and lightning. Two weeks earlier, the twenty-two-year-old had posted a video clip on the Internet about his weather fears, which had plagued him since he was a toddler. "I hate all the noise," he said. "I hate the flashes of light."

By the time his shift at Fred's ended late that afternoon, his pulse had returned to normal. There wasn't a storm cloud in the sky. Instead of heading to his apartment, he drove to his father's house to pick up a few boxes of childhood possessions that he had promised to clear out of the attic. After he loaded them in his car, his stepmother, Vicki, invited him to stay for a lasagna dinner. As soon as they had finished, Jeff's mobile phone buzzed with a text alert: "The National Weather Service has issued a TORNADO WARNING for Faulkner County." They were sitting in Faulkner County.

He and his father, Tim, looked outside and saw that the sky had turned ominous. On the television, a red-splotched radar map filled the screen. Jeff and his family didn't need the weatherman to tell them to get to safety—it sounded as if a jet were taking off on their lawn. The three of them rushed into an interior bathroom. Jeff and Vicki cowered inside the tub. Tim knelt next to them. While his dad and stepmom prayed, Jeff pulled out his phone and posted a message on Facebook: "Multi vortex tornado!!!!! Get to safety!!!"

Then he tapped out a text message. "Mama I'm so scared."

"I love you Jeff," his mother wrote back from her home twenty miles away. "You will make it."

"It's heading right for me."

Before she could respond, he sent another text.

"I love you mama . . ."

Seconds later, a quarter-mile-wide EF4 tornado touched down on Clover Ridge Drive, the street where Jeff's father lived, ripping the house apart and tearing into the bathroom. It sucked Jeff from the tub and into a ferocious funnel cloud. Neighbors found Jeff's body on the street later that evening, buried under fragments of the house and the family's possessions. Both Tim and Vicki were seriously injured, but they survived. "I have no idea how," Tim said.

As he recovered in a local hospital and grieved for Jeff, Tim worried about his house. His brother, Anthony Hunter, broke the news that it was beyond repair. Every home on Tim's side of Clover Ridge Drive had been destroyed by the tornado. Roofs were gone and windows shattered. Two-by-fours had been snapped in half as if they were matchsticks. Family photographs and heirlooms were scattered everywhere. Residents, friends, and family would have to sort through the rubble to recover whatever could be salvaged. Then the owners would have to call a demolition crew. Everything—the bricks, the floor tiles, the drywall, the appliances, the waterlogged furniture—would have to be hauled away.

Tim was certain the demolition firms would be charging top dollar, as they always did after big storms, and he feared the cost would deplete the insurance funds he would need to rebuild his house. He knew of others in Vilonia who had used so much of their insurance payouts to clear their lots after a tornado three years earlier that they were unable to afford new homes.

Anthony returned to the house the next day, driving through a tableau of postapocalyptic devastation. National Guard troops offered to help look for family keepsakes, but they couldn't dismantle the structure. As Anthony prepared to search for a wrecking crew to hire, two men pulled up in a black Ford pickup truck. Clad in matching gray T-shirts identifying them as members of Team Rubicon, they walked around the property, their boots crunching shards of glass. One took notes on a clipboard, while the other tapped on a tablet computer and took a few photographs.

They offered to demolish what remained of the house and haul the debris to the curb so it could be collected by municipal workers, for free.

"Who are you guys?" Anthony asked.

"We're veterans," one said. "We're here to help."

The morning after the tornado, Team Rubicon began mobilizing as an Army battalion might. Two scouts arrived within a day, while first responders were still searching for victims and National Guard forces were just reaching the area. The Rubicon reconnaissance team quickly determined that local authorities were capable of handling the immediate rescue effort, but the community would need assistance with everything else: fastening plastic tarpaulins over damaged roofs, chopping up fallen trees, and hauling away the detritus of the storm. Scores of families like the Hunters required several sets of hands but lacked the money to hire private cleanup crews.

Then came the advance party. Over the following three days, several more Rubicon staffers and volunteer organizers descended on the area to pitch camp, unpack computers and chain saws, coordinate the arrival of rank-and-file volunteers, and introduce themselves to local officials. Meanwhile, an assessment team drove out to talk to residents and compile work orders that would be given to Rubicon's foot soldiers.

Five days after the storm, Team Rubicon's two dozen volunteers were ready to go. They began the morning by hoisting an American flag and reciting the Pledge of Allegiance in the sunbaked parking lot of a Home Depot, where they had established their field headquarters. Many had thrown sleeping bags in their cars and driven from as far as three hundred miles away. Some were college students who had decided to skip a week of classes to help. Others were self-employed or unemployed. A few had taken vacation time off from their jobs. One enterprising woman from Oklahoma City had persuaded her boss to handle her absence the same way the firm would treat an employee's National Guard deployment—with full pay.

Joseph D'Amico, a burly former Marine turned entrepreneur, had been driving from Texas to his home in Connecticut with his fiancée, Pam Izzo, when he heard that Rubicon was responding to the tornado. He quickly diverted his Audi. He had served on a Rubicon tornado relief team a year earlier in Oklahoma and wanted to show Pam, a nurse, what it was all about. A few hours after they arrived in Arkansas, Pam had changed into a Rubicon shirt and was hauling tree branches.

Everybody on Team Rubicon was a veteran, except for Pam. Three had fought in Vietnam. The rest, all in their twenties and thirties, had served in Iraq or Afghanistan, or both. After spending years in the military taking orders, all of them had earned the right to kick back and let others do the hard work during moments of national crisis. But, motivated by television footage of the tornado's aftermath, they wanted to help. When Rubicon told its members about the opportunity to lend a hand in Arkansas, the organization restricted sign-ups to those living within two hundred miles of the storm site, to limit long drives and avoid expensive reimbursements for gasoline. The circle on the map excluded several members living in Texas and Oklahoma who were eager to participate. They received dispensation to come, if they agreed to carpool to save on gas money.

Although they didn't wear camouflage or carry weapons, Rubicon members ran the assistance effort with the same organization, expedition, and nomenclature as a military mission. Their headquarters was called the FOB—forward operating base. The command staff divided their functions as a battalion staff would, into operations, planning, communications, medical, and logistics. There was a morning brief, after which the group ate whatever chow was provided—often fried-chicken sandwiches from Chick-fil-A. They wore identical gray T-shirts, each emblazoned with their name, and divided themselves into teams named Alpha, Bravo, and Charlie, to fulfill work orders issued by the mission's commander. Before they departed from the parking lot each day, they checked out equipment from neatly organized toolsheds, cleaning and testing their chain saws as they once did M16s. At night, they slept on Army-issue cots in a warehouse. Their endeavor even had a name: Operation Rising Eagle.

On the seventh morning after the tornado, once the flag raising and fried-chicken breakfast were finished, the incident commander, Chad Reynolds, told the volunteers that the headquarters had a large pile of outstanding work requests. "We're behind the eight ball," he said. "Let's get out there and get stuff done."

Before they left, the group received a weather report—another hot, sunny day—and a warning from the health officer. "Be careful of snakes, scorpions, chiggers, and meth labs."

The Alpha team packed its pickup under the exacting eye of its leader, Randi Gavell, a petite former Army military police staff sergeant, who enforced the same standards she applied in Iraq, when her platoon's Humvees were loaded with ammunition and ready-to-eat meals. Two ladders, two chain saws, two axes. A sledgehammer and shovel for everyone. Every implement was assembled neatly in the truck bed.

They drove for twenty minutes, sitting as they would if in the Army—the junior guy behind the wheel, Gavell in the front passenger seat, and the others on the rear bench—before turning onto Clover Ridge Drive. Because every house on the block had been eviscerated and every mailbox uprooted, Gavell and the five other veterans on her team had to count their way to the eighth dwelling on the right, number 16. This was the Hunters' home.

As Gavell's team huddled on the driveway, tools in hand, she informed them that their work site was a DBS—death by storm—house. Her information was jumbled, as can often happen in the chaotic days after a disaster. She told them a six-year-old boy had been killed in the home. She didn't know—nor did anyone else at Rubicon—that Tim Hunter worked for the Arkansas National Guard. Even if they had, it wouldn't have mattered. Although Rubicon volunteers take particular pleasure in aiding fellow veterans, they triage work orders based on need, not military service.

"Yeah, it's hot and muggy and dirty, and it's hard work," Gavell told her crew. "But if you see a brick on the ground, remember that brick could have seen a child's first steps, it saw family dinners and first dates and birthdays. It saw their lives. This was their everything." Gavell urged her team to take a break if the work got too taxing or emotionally overwhelming. "You're humans. You have souls. It's going to be hard," she said.

The two burliest guys, Cody Wright and Tyler Bacon, both members of the Arkansas National Guard whose units had not been activated for storm response, swung sledgehammers at the remnants of the kitchen and master bathroom. Gavell tucked her dirty-blond hair under a white hard hat that carried a bumper sticker declaring, "Women who behave rarely make history," and began prying apart wooden cabinets with a crowbar. Others used shovels, wheelbarrows, and their gloved hands to deposit the debris in giant piles along the street, next to a red Ford Contour that had been tossed into the front yard as a child might discard a Matchbox car.

A TEAM RUBICON VOLUNTEER HELPS TO DEMOLISH THE HUNTERS' HOME

If they spotted an item that appeared to be irreplaceable—a ribbon from a sports contest, an old photograph, a piece of needlepoint—it was put aside. But everything else that had made the Hunter house a home was swept away: a Linkin Park compact disc, a bottle of rainbow-colored cake sprinkles, a package of Glade air freshener, a wooden wall clock.

Gavell encouraged her teammates to stay hydrated and take a breather when needed. But she couldn't afford to allow them to lollygag. There were dozens more houses that they needed to get to. She couldn't yell at slackers the way she did in the Army. These people were, after all, volunteers who could simply leave if they wanted. So she led by example, rarely pausing in her labor, and cajoled others to follow her lead. The old sergeant Gavell burst forth only once, when one member of her team grabbed a wooden duck from a trash pile. "We don't take anything," she admonished. "I don't care if it's garbage."

After a brief break to scarf down boxed lunches provided by church volunteers, Gavell instructed her team to remove everything from the concrete slab on which the house had been built. Otherwise, she said, county inspectors would not be able to issue the family a permit to construct a new house. So they continued hammering, shoveling, and sweeping for another two hours. When they finished, she gathered them around once again. "You guys are fucking rock stars," she gushed. "You just cleared off a path to rebuild dreams."

Team Rubicon's journey to Arkansas began with the devastating earthquake that struck Haiti in January 2010. Jacob Wood, a former Marine sniper who had witnessed no dearth of carnage in Iraq and Afghanistan, was shaken by television footage of the shattered Caribbean island nation.

This looks just like Fallujah, he thought. *I should get down there. I can make a difference.* A moment later, he checked himself. *What the fuck am I going to do? I'm one guy. Nobody will think this is a good idea.*

But Wood didn't permit prudence to scuttle his impulse. He relished challenges. He had attended the University of Wisconsin at Madison on a football scholarship, playing on the offensive line. He had thought about walking away from school just three weeks into his freshman year, right after the 9/11 attacks, but he figured it made sense to finish studying before serving. As he learned more about the wars, his desire to join the military only grew. In his junior year, that desire became resolve after reading news reports of the Marines' first campaign to retake the Iraqi town of Fallujah and after learning that Pat Tillman, who had given up a promising National Football League career to become an Army Ranger, had been killed in Afghanistan. Although most college graduates opt to become officers, Wood didn't want to wait a year—while he went through officer school and was assigned to lead a platoon— to engage in combat. So he enlisted in the Marines and became a private.

Transformed by boot camp from a beefy lineman to a chiseled infantryman, he soon found himself on the outskirts of Fallujah, but he didn't stay a buck private for long. He was a natural leader, and his intellect and thirst for action attracted quick notice. He had arrived in Iraq in charge of a four-man team; two weeks later, he was promoted to corporal and named co-leader of a squad, directing his men through near-daily ambushes and roadside bomb blasts. A year and a half later, after graduating from Marine sniper school at the top of his class, he went to southern Afghanistan for seven months.

His dangerous stint there stripped away the last of his college-student fantasies about warfare. He worried that he was growing numb to violence. By the time he returned to Camp Pendleton on the Southern California coast in 2009, he had resolved to leave the military. He traveled to South America, moved in with his girlfriend, and applied to business schools.

Then the ground shook in Haiti. He was certain he could be of help. He knew how to dig people out of rubble, he could wield a hammer and a saw, and he could live out of a backpack, sleeping under the stars, without running water or other creature comforts. *I can work in pure chaos,* he said to himself.

"I really think I should go down there," he told his girlfriend, who made him promise that he wouldn't travel alone. He called the Red Cross, which informed him that it did not encourage spontaneous volunteers. He called his buddies in California, all of whom demurred. Then he called Jeff Lang, one of his college roommates, who had become a firefighter in Milwaukee. "Sure, dude," his friend replied. "When do you want to go?" Lang said another firefighter in his station who had been a Marine wanted to join. Wood also posted a message on his Facebook page. A few hours later, he got a call from William McNulty, someone he had known in the Marines. "Wood, I want in," McNulty said.

The four men arrived in Haiti days after the quake, joining forces with two civilian physicians and a former Army Special Operations medic who also were traveling on their own and hoping to find ways to participate in relief efforts. As soon as they reached Port-au-Prince, the group saw how vast the problems were. They focused on providing emergency medical assistance, which seemed to be the most urgent need.

As word of their work reached home, their e-mail in-boxes began filling with queries of interest. Within two weeks, their ranks grew to thirty, most of them veterans. Among the new arrivals was one of Wood's closest friends, Clay Hunt, a Marine who had served in his platoon in Fallujah. Hunt had been shot by a sniper and had lost two of his platoon mates to attacks. He was struggling with post-traumatic stress, depression, and an unraveling marriage. Throwing himself into humanitarian aid appeared to brighten his mood. As the group returned home after a month, McNulty suggested to Wood that they organize a repeat performance when the next natural disaster struck overseas. "We can make it like a club," Wood replied.

Over the following year, their "club," which they called Team Rubicon, headed to tsunami-ravaged Chile, Burma, South Sudan,

and flood-stricken parts of Pakistan. Other veterans who participated told Wood and McNulty that the relief operations were the
most meaningful work they had performed since leaving the military. Several said the overseas trips gave them a sense of purpose as
they struggled to build post-military lives and cope with the after-
effects of combat.

In early 2011, Wood and McNulty began talking about how
they could expand their group to help more disaster victims, as well
as veterans. That March, the handsome and gregarious Hunt, who
had met with members of Congress and appeared in public-service
videos made by the Iraq and Afghanistan Veterans of America to
raise awareness about post-traumatic stress, locked himself in his
Houston apartment and shot himself. Hunt's suicide was a devastating blow to Wood. The two had gone to sniper school together
and deployed to Afghanistan in the same unit. Wood had been
the best man at Hunt's wedding. Instead of the pills prescribed to
Hunt by his VA doctor, which didn't seem to work, Wood wished
he could have doled out the same sense of purpose Hunt felt when
he trudged through the slums of Port-au-Prince.

A few weeks after Hunt's funeral, a tornado walloped Tusca-
loosa, Alabama. Until then, Wood hadn't focused on domestic
disaster relief, but he decided to put out the call to his volunteers.
Three days into the Alabama operation, as he sat around a campfire
and drank whiskey with fifteen other veteran volunteers late on a
Sunday night, he heard President Obama would be making a major
national security announcement within the hour. Over the radio
he learned that Osama bin Laden had been killed by Navy SEALs.
Wood took it as a sign. Clay Hunt was dead. Osama was dead. The
war had shifted to the home front. He had to do all he could for
his fellow veterans. He wondered if he could mobilize even more
veterans for projects within the United States.

A month later, Rubicon volunteers descended on Joplin, Missouri, after the town was struck by a gargantuan tornado. Then came Hurricane Sandy on the East Coast. The organization deployed three hundred veterans, running operations in New York and New Jersey for six weeks. By the time the tornado that killed Jeff Hunter struck central Arkansas, Rubicon had conducted nearly sixty operations and grown to sixteen thousand volunteers, divided into ten domestic zones that mirror the Federal Emergency Management Agency's regional structure.

The volunteers ranged from former commandos who couldn't talk about the secret missions they conducted to young National Guard troops who performed the menial chores of war. The Joplin operation drew an Air Force intelligence analyst, a chemical-warfare specialist, and a Navy submarine technician. The three Vietnam veterans who joined the Arkansas operation weren't unusual. Most relief efforts attracted a few fit graybeards who wanted to toil next to their Iraq and Afghanistan brethren. "I have yet to find a Vietnam veteran who hasn't said, 'I wish you were around forty years ago when I came home,'" Wood said.

For every case of post-traumatic stress among veterans, Wood was convinced there was a case of post-traumatic growth—sometimes in the same person. Every Rubicon operation brought a few men and women who had folded up their uniforms and felt rudderless in the civilian world. They found rejuvenation in aiding others. The gray T-shirts, the backbreaking labor, the austere accommodations, unappealing as they might have seemed to many nonveterans, were a throwback to veterans' glory days. And their work exposed a nation disconnected from its military to the spirit of service that motivated so many young men and women to wear the uniform.

"There's a value and power of continued service—for veterans and for society as a whole," Wood said. "We can be an example of what the next greatest generation can be."

=★=

Randi Gavell, the former sergeant who led the cleanup of the Hunters' home, was among those who had traveled to Arkansas seeking to help storm victims even as she sought to find a way forward herself.

She had joined the Army fresh out of high school in Grand Junction, Colorado. She became a military police soldier and two years later, in 2005, was sent to Iraq. Stationed in the chaotic western city of Ramadi, on the grounds of a water-treatment plant next to the Euphrates River, her unit was tasked with training Iraqi policemen. There were plenty of young men in Ramadi willing to sign up and claim a paycheck, but getting them to show up for duty and patrol the streets proved far more difficult.

Although there were multiple attacks against American troops in Ramadi, Gavell never felt anxious until one morning in August 2006 when rain fell from the sky. Residents rejoiced at this most unusual sight in the Iraqi desert, but Gavell didn't. "A bad omen," she warned her comrades.

An hour later, three trucks laden with explosives roared toward the front gate of the water plant. The first suicide bomber intended to detonate next to the gate, allowing the other two to drive inside before exploding, in an attempt to flatten the structure and maximize casualties. But the first truck exploded prematurely, triggering the other two vehicles and creating a massive fireball that incinerated two dozen recruits waiting outside. Ten of the twelve American soldiers inside the compound were injured, including Gavell, who suffered a severe concussion and a blown-out right eardrum.

Then came post-traumatic stress—blurred vision, bouts of dizziness, insomnia, and headaches so painful that she couldn't get out of bed. Her Army doctor pumped her full of medicine—as many as thirty prescription pills a day, including a drug designed to treat testicular cancer that he thought would ease her anxiety. The pills numbed her aches and helped her sleep, but she spent her daytime hours in a haze.

After two years, she decided to quit taking the drugs cold turkey. "You lose so much of yourself anyway; I didn't want to lose the rest of myself to the pills," she said. The decision cost her her military career. She couldn't keep serving if she had to call in sick once or twice a week on the days when she lay in bed curled up and shaking from migraines.

She eventually turned to exercise as a salve. She participated in the U.S. Olympic Committee's inaugural Warrior Games for wounded service members and veterans, competing in swimming and volleyball. When she got out of the Army in 2010, she moved to Los Angeles, climbed on a bicycle, and joined a group called Ride 2 Recovery. As she became involved with the organization, she struck up a conversation with a fellow veteran struggling with post-traumatic stress, Clay Hunt.

They became fast friends. When he visited Southern California, he stayed in her apartment, and they commiserated about the challenges in adjusting to civilian life. On one visit, as he took a break from playing his guitar, he talked about his international aid work and urged her to sign up for Team Rubicon.

His suicide left Gavell despondent. She copied a tattoo he'd had on his arm onto her wrist: "Not all who wander are lost." And she began to doubt her own recovery. If Clay, who had seemed so strong, felt so helpless, would she follow the same path? She tried to move forward. She met a woman at a Ride 2 Recovery race who introduced Gavell to her brother. They got engaged. For a while, it appeared that she was going to be okay. By the spring of 2013, however, the engagement had hit the skids. She had moved to Colorado, he to Hawaii. She wished Clay were still around; he was always the one to get her back on her feet.

"When you get out, you don't realize how lost you'll be," she said. She tried to go to college but felt awkward as a freshman at twenty-five. She took physical education and art classes at a community college but found them unfulfilling. She tried business courses, but they were too difficult and boring. She tried online education, but she lacked the discipline to complete the course work. She moved to Hawaii to attend massage therapy school and rekindle her engagement, but both ventures failed, and she eventually returned to Colorado.

That May, as she was wallowing in depression, a giant tornado struck Moore, Oklahoma. A day later, she received an e-mail from Team Rubicon asking if she'd be interested in participating in the relief operation. "It felt like Clay was telling me to go," she recalled.

So she did, first for a week, then for a month. She reveled in the grueling work, in the opportunity to help people, in the camaraderie. It was Army life, minus the insurgents. A year later, when the tornado hit central Arkansas, she readily agreed to join the operation from her new home in Oklahoma City. "For me, helping other people is how I help myself," she said. "This is therapeutic. It's the best kind of medicine there is. I don't need all of those pills if I can come and give hope to someone."

The night before she led the team to clear out the Hunters' lot, she was struck with a migraine. She didn't sleep more than an hour. The next morning, although she projected a calm and disciplined demeanor, the lack of rest caught up with her. She forgot to deliver a safety briefing to her team until midday. But once they finished at the Hunters' and moved on to a house whose roof had been smashed by a falling tree, which required her team to bring out the chain saws, she had regained her focus. Anyone using a saw, she insisted, had to wear a hard hat, goggles, and bright orange safety chaps.

She hoisted herself onto the roof carrying a tarp and a bucket of nails to seal the opening. Then she grabbed an ax and began splitting logs from the fallen tree. It wasn't a service Rubicon typically performed, but Gavell knew that Maxine Coughlin, the seventy-three-year-old widow who lived in the house, depended on firewood to keep warm in the winter, and there was no way she could chop the logs herself.

Gavell split log after log in a gully next to Coughlin's garage, working herself into a frenzy. Her breath quickened and sweat dripped onto a pink bandana under her hard hat, but she refused to stop until the entire forty-foot-tall tree had been divvied up into chunks of firewood.

When she finally put down the ax, she noticed a faded and tattered American flag next to Coughlin's door. The following morning, Gavell returned with a new one and presented it to Coughlin. The gray-haired woman embraced Gavell, and they chatted on her stoop.

Coughlin explained that her late husband, who had been captured by Chinese forces during the Korean War, had insisted upon displaying the Stars and Stripes in front of their house. The flag was his, and she had kept it flying, despite its threadbare condition, to honor him.

Gavell told her she didn't need to remove it, that she could keep the replacement inside the house. But Coughlin said she wanted to display the new one to honor the young veterans who had covered her roof, cut her trees, and chopped her wood. She pointed at members of Gavell's team.

"After everything you have been through in the wars, you still want to help people," she said. "All of you make us proud to be Americans."

CHAPTER EIGHT

Something Positive Has to Come from This

When the first medical evacuation flight from the Iraq war arrived at Camp Pendleton in early April 2003, the commander of the base hospital walked up to Karen Guenther and said, "Help me welcome these heroes back." Guenther, a civilian nurse in the pediatric unit, figured she would applaud, say "Get well soon!" and then get back to work.

Over the next few days, though, she saw that the base wasn't sufficiently prepared for the wives and children and mothers and fathers of the wounded. The relatives had come in haste upon being notified that their loved one was on the way to Pendleton, not taking time to prepare for their temporary relocation. The cost of staying in hotels in the Southern California beach communities near the Marine base meant some families only had enough money left over to eat one meal a day. Others had taken to sleeping in their cars.

Guenther, an energetic California native whose husband was among the twenty-five thousand Marines advancing on Baghdad, was appalled. *We should be better than this,* she thought. She knew that trying to persuade the military bureaucracy to provide the families with increased financial assistance could take months or even years. So she called several fellow Marine wives and invited them to join her in assembling bags of clothing, toiletries, and children's toys. They asked local restaurants for gift certificates and cobbled together donations to buy telephone calling cards.

Not long after, her nursing supervisor told her that she had seen a young wife who weighed no more than 120 pounds trying to lift her quadriplegic Marine husband into a Chevy Blazer. At the time, the military did not provide funds for wounded troops to buy handicap-enabled vehicles, and the couple couldn't afford one on their own. The supervisor knew of Guenther's previous work for the families. "Karen, can you help?" she asked.

Guenther made some calls and eventually found the Nice Guys of San Diego, a nonprofit organization that had long assisted military spouses in the area with household problems while their husbands were away. The Nice Guys readily agreed to raise money to buy a vehicle with hand controls and a wheelchair lift. Two weeks later, she and some of the Nice Guys delivered a van to the paralyzed Marine and his wife. She handed over the keys in the presence of doctors and nurses from the hospital, many of whom cried with joy.

As word of the van spread, Guenther's phone started to ring incessantly. The voices on the other end were those not of Marines and their relatives—most didn't know how to reach her—but of doctors, nurses, and battalion commanders who had learned of a pressing need and hoped she could play angel. *These families really need our help,* she soon realized.

Most of the requests were for assistance the military couldn't or wouldn't provide. Spouses and children were reimbursed for airplane tickets to the cities where wounded Marines had been taken for hospitalization, but the government didn't pay the travel expenses of girlfriends or boyfriends and siblings. The same policy applied to hotels and food stipends. Some families found themselves unable to make mortgage and car payments because wives had quit their jobs to care for their injured husbands. When troops were well enough to return home, their houses and apartments had to be retrofitted with wheelchair ramps and new bathrooms.

Guenther contacted the spouses who had helped her collect clothes and other donated items, three of whom were generals' wives. She said there was more work to be done. Guenther's husband was only a major, and in the rank-conscious world of military spouses, the others could have sought to take charge. But Karen was so enthusiastic and full of ideas that she was encouraged by the others to stay in the lead.

"We knew that if this was going to succeed, it would require Karen's energy and her love of people," said Bonnie Amos, whose husband, Jim, was a two-star general at the time.

The women decided to establish a not-for-profit organization called the Injured Marine Semper Fi Fund, paying homage to the Corps' motto: *Semper fidelis,* "Always faithful." None of them had any business experience. At the first meeting, held around Guenther's dining table, she wrote three words in block letters in her notebook: KEEP IT SIMPLE. Her next act was to read the book *Nonprofit Kit for Dummies,* then a few more relevant books. Aiding troops hurt in Iraq "became a personal quest," she recalled. "Our husbands were there."

The spouses agreed to keep their efforts focused on providing the sort of financial assistance the military wasn't offering. They avoided projects that duplicated what the Defense Department and the Department of Veterans Affairs were obligated to fund.

They also brought a streamlined approach to doling out their grants. Instead of asking Marines and their relatives to fill out lengthy forms and then sorting through applications to decide which ones to approve, the spouses relied on recommendations from commanders and senior noncommissioned officers, doctors and nurses, and military social workers. Because generals' wives were involved, those submitting nominations took care to raise only the most deserving cases. The system allowed the Semper Fi Fund to hand out assistance rapidly.

"We refused to say, 'Let's review your application. We'll get back to you in six months,'" Guenther said. "We don't have to do research to know what the needs are." Emergency cases, she said, could be dealt with in hours, and routine cases could be handled in days. "It started that way, and it's still that way."

One Sunday morning soon after the fund had been established, Guenther received a phone call from a battalion commander who was a friend of her husband's. He told her that four Marines had been wounded in a training accident and that their families were headed to the base. The military would pay for hotel rooms, but there wasn't anyone working that day who could handle the paperwork. Guenther offered to cover the costs of the rooms with the fund's credit card.

As the fund attracted attention and donors—much of its early support came in the form of small checks written by active and retired service members—senior officers in the Pentagon openly wondered whether a group of spouses was capable of running what was turning into a nationwide charity. The wives faced the challenge of moving every two years. Could the fund operate effectively, the officers asked, when the dinner-table group at Pendleton scattered to Marine bases in North Carolina, Virginia, and Okinawa?

Yes, Guenther answered. The women would use e-mail and Skype to run the organization. Besides, she argued, spreading out would allow the group to identify new people to assist and new sources of revenue. "We had the passion," she said. "That overshadowed the fact that we didn't have MBAs."

Over the following decade, the fund went on to raise and disburse more than ninety million dollars. "Now I have MBAs from Harvard and Yale calling and asking me, 'How have you done this?'" Guenther said.

The spouses' business practices won over the early doubters in Washington—and deep-pocketed donors across the nation. The fund didn't rely on mass mailings and television ads, instead operating primarily on word of mouth in the tight-knit world of active-duty and former Marines. Overhead costs—what it paid in salaries and fund-raising expenses—remained at less than 6 percent of revenue, which earned the group a coveted A-plus rating from the American Institute of Philanthropy. That endorsement, in turn, led to a tide of donations from people the wives had never solicited, allowing the Semper Fi Fund to handle hundreds of cases a month as the Iraq war worsened.

Among those they aided was Merlin German, a Marine who had been burned over 97 percent of his body by a gas-fed roadside bomb and who miraculously clung to life. The fund helped to pay the bills so his mother, Lourdes, could sit by his bedside for seventeen months at the Brooke Army Medical Center near San Antonio. As he convalesced, he'd walk into the rooms of other patients—nobody there was as severely burned—and say, "Hey, what's wrong with you? Time to get up." Although he recovered enough to leave the hospital, he died three years after the blast from complications resulting from a skin graft surgery.

Ronny Porta was another Marine who was badly burned by a roadside bomb. He underwent more than 120 surgeries. The fund stepped in to allow his immigrant family to make his recovery their full-time job, compensating them for their lost wages. When Porta was well enough to live at home with his wife and young son, the fund paid for improvements to his house, including a shower that minimizes pressure on his skin and a computer that he can command with his voice.

Not all of the Semper Fi Fund's cases involved war wounds. Guenther learned of a young lance corporal dying of leukemia at the Naval Medical Center in San Diego. He was alone because his migrant-farmworker parents, who had to feed five other children, couldn't afford to leave their jobs. Guenther asked the fund's board for dispensation to help. Within a week, the organization had established a new program to assist severely ill Marines and their families.

Although profound needs among Marine and Navy families—and limited funds to disburse—initially led Guenther and the board to restrict their work to those two services, it pained her and her caseworkers to walk into military hospitals and not be able to help the parents of Army soldiers. She discovered there was no analogue to aid Army and Air Force families. "Sitting in the ICU waiting room, you would be talking to the mom of a Marine. Next to her is a mom of a soldier. How do you say, 'I can help *you*, but I can't help *you*'? It killed us not to be able to write them a check."

In 2011, a donor offered one million dollars to create a new initiative to assist non-Marines and their families. Guenther called it America's Fund. Interservice rivalry was cast aside. Guenther and her staff embraced the soldiers as warmly as they did Marines. That's how they wound up helping Jessica and Flip Klein.

Jess Klein was opening a Panera Bread café in Tacoma, Washington, where she worked as a manager, when her mobile phone rang. On the screen was an international number that she did not recognize. She picked up anyway. Her husband, Flip, a captain in the Army, was deployed to southern Afghanistan, and sometimes his calls home showed up as unusual numbers.

"Mrs. Klein?"

"Oh, shit," Jess responded. "Is he dead?"

"No, but . . ."

The voice on the other end, a nurse at the main trauma center in Kandahar, began listing Flip's injuries. Both of his legs had been blown off. His right arm was gone. His pelvis was crushed, and he had a burst femoral artery.

Jess collapsed. A colleague put her in a chair. Another employee drove her home. Jess called Flip's mom and her father. Then she rang the wife of the executive officer in Flip's battalion. "I'm in trouble," Jess said through tears.

When Flip had headed to Afghanistan in the fall of 2012, he and Jess had talked briefly about what would happen if he died. He wanted to be buried in his family's plot in North Carolina. They hadn't discussed the prospect of a severe injury. *He's going to be fine,* Jess had thought. *Nothing bad is going to happen to my husband.*

Flip and Jess had met at West Point in 2002, when both were first-year cadets. She had been raised in Texas by parents who served in the military. Her mother was an Army chief warrant officer, her father an Air Force master sergeant, and she knew from a young age that she, too, wanted to join the military. She applied to West Point, believing that "it was the last bastion of all that was good in the world."

Flip, who is four years older, arrived there circuitously. He had attended Texas Christian University, where he played football, but dropped out after three semesters. After bouncing around and skirting the edge of trouble, in 2000 he decided to enlist in the Army. He survived boot camp and airborne school and was then sent to complete signals intelligence training at Goodfellow Air Force Base in San Angelo, Texas. He continued to push the boundaries, enough so that a chief warrant officer regularly had to discipline him.

The following year, Flip deployed to Kuwait. After the September 11 attacks, he was assigned to help collect intelligence for the impending war in Afghanistan. While there, his older brother, who had attended West Point, urged him to apply to the academy as well. Flip, then a lowly private, scrawled out an application with a pen while sitting on a bench in the Kuwaiti desert. When he was accepted, he agonized for days over whether to actually attend. One evening, he worked his way through a case of Budweiser trying to decide. The next morning, he asked his roommate if he had seen the school's reply card lying around. "Yeah," he said. "You got pretty hammered, and at one o'clock you said, 'Fuck it, I'm going to mail the damn thing.'" And he had.

Because Flip was a few years older than most in his class and was already familiar with Army life, he became one of two informal leaders of his cadet group. The other was Jess, a petite brunette who had experienced the rigors of military life at home and was able to master the memorization tests upperclassmen used to haze the new kids. Flip and Jess became friends, and then more. After their first year, Jess decided that West Point wasn't for her and instead chose to pursue a degree in mechanical engineering at the University of Texas at San Antonio. But she held on to Flip.

She figured he should meet her parents, so he flew to west Texas, a bottle of bourbon in hand, and knocked on their door. When her mother opened it, he saw the same chief warrant officer who had disciplined him at Goodfellow. "Oh, fuck," he muttered. "It's you."

After a laugh, he began to see Jess's mother in a new light, not merely as a future in-law or a strict boss, but as a source of insight. He'd stay up late with Jess's parents, long after she had gone to bed, to talk with them about their military service.

Flip and Jess married a week after his graduation in 2006. He deployed to Iraq in 2007 as a platoon leader in the 101st Airborne Division, spending fifteen months in an insurgent stronghold known as the Triangle of Death. Upon his return, he thought about leaving the Army, but there were still two items on his military to-do list: he wanted to serve in Afghanistan, and he wanted to lead a company of infantrymen. He got his first wish in April 2012, when he headed to Afghanistan with the Second Infantry Division as a battalion staff officer. In September of that year, he got his second wish, when he was given command of a company in the Second Brigade combat team with 170 soldiers and twenty armored Stryker vehicles. They were responsible for about fourteen square miles of farmland west of Kandahar city.

On October 22, he set out with one of his platoons on a foot patrol to inspect a cluster of mud-walled houses that were believed to be Taliban bomb factories. The goal, he told his men, was "to poke the hornet's nest." Flip, who retained his football physique and topped the scales at 210 pounds, followed a path that had been trod by a bomb-sniffing dog and a soldier with a metal detector. Perhaps it was his weight, or perhaps, as he put it, "it was my time," but he suddenly found himself propelled into the air.

He landed in a cloud of dust, hearing the thunderclap of a detonated antipersonnel mine—a three-quart plastic jug packed with homemade explosives—reverberating across the Arghandab River valley. The platoon's medic, Specialist Drew Evans, rushed up to him and began strapping on tourniquets, eight in all—one on what was left of each of his four limbs, two around his upper thighs, and two around his pelvis. Evans didn't tell Flip how badly he had been wounded, and Flip wasn't concentrating on his injuries. Worried that the blast might be followed by an ambush, he directed his troops into a defensive position. He wanted to know where his snipers were and asked to get on the radio. A senior sergeant in the company finally told him, "You need to focus on yourself, sir."

Flip's medical evacuation helicopter touched down at the Kandahar airport trauma center forty-five minutes later. Amputating his legs and right arm was the easiest part of his initial surgery. The damage to his organs and pelvis and the effects of blood loss had left him on the brink of death. It took the doctors three days to stabilize him enough to put him on an air-ambulance flight to a military hospital in Germany. Even then, he had to be pulled off for a day when the plane stopped at another base in Afghanistan; his vital signs had crashed. For a few moments, doctors on board thought he had died.

When he finally made it to Germany, Jess thought he'd be heading to an Army hospital in the United States within a day. But Hurricane Sandy was then smacking the East Coast. When Flip eventually arrived five days later, unconscious and connected to a ventilator, his face puffy from massive doses of steroids and fluids, Jess was elated.

"It didn't even occur to me not to be happy," she recalled. "He was alive. The rest we could get through."

Flip spent his first month at the Walter Reed National Military Medical Center in the intensive-care unit, suffering through almost-daily surgeries and fending off infections. Jess was there every day, either sitting next to his bed with her hand on his head or balled up in the third-floor waiting room, shivering from the November chill. She had left home in a rush, not thinking about packing for winter in Maryland, and she wasn't about to leave the hospital to go shopping for warm clothes.

As soon as one of Guenther's case managers, Karen Hetherington, saw Jess in the waiting room, she excused herself and returned with an armful of fleece blankets and jackets. Hetherington held Jess's hand and asked just one question: "What can we do for you?" Because the Fisher House at Walter Reed, a nonprofit that provides housing to families of hospital patients, was full, Jess was staying at a nearby Marriott hotel, and she had to drive a rental car back and forth. With her life uprooted, she yearned for the familiarity of her own steering wheel. She had asked the Army to ship her Jeep Grand Cherokee from Washington State, noting that it would be cheaper than to continue renting a car for her, because

Flip faced a long stay at Walter Reed, but the Army refused because it had not formally relocated him. When Jess explained all that, Hetherington said, "Don't worry." Two weeks later, Jess had her Jeep.

During the first three months Flip was at Walter Reed, Jess woke up every day not knowing if he'd survive the next twenty-four hours. His limb stumps began to heal, and he regained consciousness on Election Day. When told what day it was, he mouthed his first words, "Who won?" But he kept losing weight. His physicians grew alarmed as the once strapping football player dropped to seventy-three pounds. In late January 2013, doctors discovered and removed a previously undetected intestinal obstruction. Within days, Flip began to improve.

More than a few young wives, married for a month or two before their husbands deployed, did not stick around once their spouses returned with grave injuries. Jess wasn't about to abandon Flip, whom she had known for a decade. Nor did she consider going back to work and leaving Flip's care to nurses and home health aides. "I needed to feel like part of the solution, rather than a bystander," she said. "Nobody is going to take better care of my husband than I am."

So Jess embraced the project of his recovery with the same gusto she brought to everything else in life. She joined the nurses and spent three hours changing the dressings on his wounds. She taught herself about every drug administered to him in order to double-check what the orderlies brought. She learned how to swap out his colostomy bags. When she and Flip moved out of the ward and into an apartment on the hospital grounds, she shaved and bathed him, took him to the bathroom, and lifted him from his wheelchair into bed.

Despite his wife's tireless assistance, Flip wanted to become self-sufficient. Using his three remaining fingers, he rolled his electric

FLIP AND JESSICA KLEIN

wheelchair to Walter Reed's rehabilitation center every morning, where he exercised his left arm, pushing himself a little further each day. He learned how to brush his teeth and shower by himself and to drive in a wheelchair-accessible vehicle. As he healed, he received prosthetic limbs and began the arduous process of trying to walk again. In between his physical therapy sessions, Flip returned to the operating room for skin grafts, pelvic reconstruction, and a procedure to rebuild his buttocks to ease the pain of sitting in a wheelchair. After undergoing a hundred surgeries, he stopped counting.

When he wasn't working out or getting worked on by doctors, Flip would roll into the rooms of newer patients. As an Army captain and a triple amputee, he commanded respect and even awe from others in the ward. He talked to them, trying to buck up their spirits, and encouraged them to get out of bed. For her part, Jess struck up conversations with the wounded men's wives and mothers, offering tips about how to navigate the hospital bureaucracy, where to eat outside the medical center campus, and what to do for some necessary relaxation. She invited some of them to join her for a manicure or a drink in downtown Bethesda, preaching what she had been unwilling to accept herself in the initial weeks after Flip's injury: that caregivers need breaks.

In the spring of 2014, Flip and Jess wanted to leave their hospital apartment—their eighty-pound dogs weren't allowed in it—and move into a nearby house so he could continue outpatient therapy, but none of the rental homes they visited were suitable for a wheelchair. Jess casually mentioned the challenge to Hetherington, who could not resist trying to help. Hetherington offered to have the Semper Fi Fund pay for the construction of ramps and bathroom handrails. That pledge allowed the couple to move into a brick rambler in a woodsy neighborhood fifteen miles north of Walter Reed.

As Flip became more independent, Jess could have gone back to the food-service industry, pursued an engineering job, or stayed at home—there was still plenty to do to care for him. Instead, she threw herself into helping other families at Walter Reed. She joined the Yellow Ribbon Fund, a nonprofit based in the Washington, D.C., area that provides services similar to the Semper Fi Fund. Her job involved helping to care for families, but with a twist: instead of focusing on housing, food, and travel, her mission was to give spouses and parents a chance to decompress. She organized pottery and cooking classes, yoga and dancing lessons, and trips to an indoor trapeze studio.

"I had forgotten what fun was," one participant gushed.

"That's the whole point," Jess replied.

Jess also organized monthly outings for a few fellow Walter Reed spouses—on her volition, not through Yellow Ribbon—that were part girls' night out, part group therapy. These evenings, which she called her "country mouse adventure club," taught younger wives that they could still get dressed up and have an occasional evening of fun, even if much of the conversation consisted of graphic descriptions of medical procedures and indecipherable military acronyms. They passed around their mobile phones to show photographs of their husbands' wounds while sharing tips about which bandages and ointments they preferred. "If the police looked at the photos on our phones, they'd think we were serial killers," Jess said.

On a Monday evening a few months after Flip and Jess moved off the hospital grounds, she hosted a dinner at an upscale tapas restaurant in Bethesda. The evening began with pink drinks and the sort of discussion young women might have at any bar in America. Jess, who had stopped at a Lululemon Athletica shop on the way, raised her gym-sculpted arms and showed off a pair of exercise pants she had purchased. Kelby Timoney, whom Jess had met in the ICU waiting room, described going back home to Oklahoma for a friend's wedding only to discover that it had been canceled. "But we had a hell of a party," she said.

As plates of finely sliced Spanish ham and chicken croquettes arrived at the table, the conversation switched to weightier topics. The women complained about cutbacks in government compensation to spousal caregivers and what appeared to be an arbitrary approach to reducing Army personnel devoted to patient care.

"They're cutting the wrong things," Jess said.

"It could be worse," Kelby shot back.

They expressed outrage that soldiers assigned to the warrior transition battalion got extra time off work—"respite days," the Army calls it—to prevent burnout.

"Are you kidding me?" Jess growled. "They work eight-hour days. What about us?"

A few sips of wine later, she confided to Kelby, "My life would be so much easier if Flip had died. But I wouldn't trade him for the world."

It was a statement, she said, she could never make in the hospital. But she knew Kelby could empathize. Her husband, Ryan, had been attacked by a suicide bomber. Ball bearings implanted in his brain affected his speech, memory, and motor skills. He had a hole in his skull covered with a titanium plate.

As difficult as it has been, Jess reminded Kelby, savor the time "at the top of the bell curve," when our husbands possess the strength to function relatively independently. In twenty years or so, Jess noted, "it's gonna go back down to him needing much more help than he needs now."

To lighten the mood, Jess listed the events she had organized the following week for spouses—another cooking class, more trapeze, and a pole-dancing session she called "vertical fitness."

"It really is amazing," Kelby said, "that given everything you do for Flip, you find the time to help so many other people."

Jess's eyes turned bashful. "Something positive has to come from this," she said. "People have been so good to us. Now we have to make it better for someone else."

Karen Guenther has seen that spirit animate not just families of the wounded but veterans themselves.

As soon as Gabriel Martinez saw the first television news reports of the Boston Marathon bombing in 2013, he sent a text message to Guenther: "We have to go to Boston. We can help them."

Martinez, a former Marine combat engineer, had lost both of his legs to a mine in southern Afghanistan on Thanksgiving Day 2010. Before his medical evacuation flight had reached the United States, a caseworker from the Semper Fi Fund had contacted his wife and mother, offering transportation assistance to the naval hospital in Bethesda for family members not covered by the military. The pledge allowed his four siblings to surprise him in the hospital. He met Guenther at a fund-raising dinner a few months after his injury. She parried his expressions of thanks, insisting instead that it was he who deserved her appreciation for his service to the Marine Corps—and the nation.

He told Guenther, in a series of texts, that he wanted to share the story of his recovery with Boston Marathon victims, several of whom had lost limbs in the blast. He wanted to tell them they could be like him: not just walking again, but running; not just running, but sprinting in competitive races. The next day, Guenther texted Martinez with an answer: "We're going to do this."

Four other veterans joined Guenther, Martinez, and a Semper Fi Fund staff member on a trip to Boston four days after the bombing: a former Marine captain who lost a leg, an eye, and several fingers to a bomb in Afghanistan; another Marine veteran whose leg was blown off in Iraq; a sailor whose leg was amputated because of an illness; and a sailor who became a paraplegic after a vehicle accident.

They visited five hospitals, starting with Massachusetts General, where many of the most severely wounded at the marathon were taken. Next up was the Boston Medical Center, where Guenther's group was greeted by a trauma specialist who was a colonel in the Army Reserve and was familiar with the fund's work. The doctor showed them around the hospital but said he could not take them into patients' rooms without consent. As the group loitered in the lobby, they began chatting up relatives of the injured. Before long, the veterans were invited into the rooms.

When Martinez heard that one of the victims had lost both of her legs—one above the knee, the other below—he told Guenther and his fellow veterans, "I have to see that person." Martinez had suffered the same type of amputations.

Martinez led the way in, finding Celeste Corcoran, a forty-seven-year-old hairdresser, and her daughter, Sydney. They had been standing on Boylston Street, near the finish line, to cheer on Celeste's sister, who was running in the race. They were less than ten feet away from one of the two pressure-cooker bombs that tore through the crowd. Celeste lost both of her legs, surviving only because her husband, Kevin, had used his belt as a tourniquet. Sydney was pelted with shrapnel, which severed her femoral artery, and she had nearly bled to death.

Both women wore blue hospital gowns. Celeste lay in bed, her brown hair pulled behind her head. Sydney sat in a reclining chair next to her.

Martinez had donned athletic shorts in order to show off his prosthetics. After brief introductions, he looked Celeste in the eyes and said, "I'm just like you."

Celeste began to cry. "I can't do anything now," she sobbed.

"Right now, yes," Martinez said. "But I'm telling you, with all my heart, you're going to be more independent than you ever were."

Cameron West, the Marine captain who lost a leg in Afghanistan, leaned over her bed and placed his hand over the empty space where her legs used to be.

"This doesn't matter," he said. "This is just a change of scenery. It really is. I mean Gabe here, he's moving and running, he's doing the Paralympics, and you know what, you may want to do that some day."

"This isn't the end," Martinez said. "This is the beginning."

CHAPTER NINE

Still Fighting for His Troops

Soon after Peter Chiarelli became vice chief of staff of the Army in 2008, a subordinate showed him a bar graph depicting the number of soldiers determined by the Department of Veterans Affairs to be at least 30 percent disabled. The tallest column was on the far left.

Those are amputations, Chiarelli thought. *Or burns.*

Then he examined the graph more carefully. Burns were off to the right, accounting for just 2 percent of disabled soldiers. Amputations were in the middle, at 10 percent. The big column, which represented 36 percent of seriously injured soldiers, was labeled "PTSD or TBI."

When Chiarelli looked mystified, the subordinate explained. PTSD, or post-traumatic stress disorder, is the catchall term to explain the anxiety, anger, and disorientation people can experience after exposure to physical harm or the threat of it. An insurgent attack would qualify, as would the threat of one, which most troops in Iraq faced every day. TBI, or traumatic brain injury, can happen when a soldier suffers a concussion from the blast of a roadside bomb. While some soldiers appeared to recover from concussions quickly, for others the effects lingered for months, or even indefinitely.

Chiarelli was dumbfounded. He had been the operational commander of all American ground forces in Iraq. Before that, he'd led an Army division that was responsible for Baghdad. And yet all this was news to him. He had assumed that the stress of a near miss would dissipate. So, too, would the effects of a concussion. He figured they were no big deal.

"If I had a platoon that lost folks, I had combat-stress teams, and I made sure they were flown to whatever base they needed to go to," he said. "I knew what my football coach told me about traumatic brain injury: 'Shake it off and get back in the game.'"

The graph sobered him. As vice-chief, his job wasn't to focus on war strategy. He was responsible for "the force"—for training and equipping soldiers, modernizing weapons and overseeing the budget, and ensuring the well-being of the half-million men and women in the Army, the second-largest U.S. employer after Walmart. But it also was personal: he had put many of these soldiers in harm's way in Iraq, and he believed he had a duty to those who returned harmed.

So Chiarelli set out to learn everything he could about PTSD and TBI. The task took on even greater urgency a month later, when the Army tallied that 115 soldiers had committed suicide in 2007. That was the most since the Army began counting in 1980 and nearly twice the national suicide rate. Chiarelli's boss, General George Casey Jr., asked him to figure out why so many soldiers were taking their own lives.

Chiarelli could see that PTSD, TBI, and military suicide were overlapping circles. But by how much? Not every soldier with a concussion was going to experience post-traumatic stress. Many stressed-out soldiers had not been subjected to explosions. And when it came to suicides, TBI did not appear to be a main cause. But all of it fit under the rubric of mental health, an issue that had never really been on the front burner at the Pentagon.

Despite failures at Walter Reed and other Army hospitals early in the Afghanistan and Iraq wars, the military was providing extraordinary care to troops who had been burned, absorbed bullets or shrapnel, or lost limbs. (The Department of Veterans Affairs, which treats those who have left active service, was a deeply troubled institution that would be accused in 2014 of falsifying patient-care records.) The advancements in prosthetics and limb transplants since 2001 had been, in Chiarelli's view, "nothing short of amazing." But he soon discovered the same couldn't be said for mental health and brain injuries. "What we were doing for their minds wasn't a tenth of what we were doing for their arms and legs," he said.

The broad-shouldered Chiarelli, whose face bore the worry lines of a general who had written too many condolence letters, summoned two military doctors, one an expert on PTSD, the other on TBI. He met with each for two hours. Then he went to Walter Reed and talked to physicians there. What they told him about the severity of the problem differed from what he had heard from the first two doctors. Frustrated, he contacted one of the few civilian doctors he knew, an accomplished plastic surgeon in Los Angeles who was providing advanced reconstruction treatment to soldiers disfigured by explosions. That doctor connected Chiarelli with David Hovda, the director of UCLA's Brain Injury Research Center, who agreed to speak with a group of military doctors at the Pentagon.

Hovda began his presentation by projecting a slide of three brain scans. The one on the right, filled with splotches of yellow and red to indicate healthy activity, was of an uninjured person. On the other two slides, instead of yellow and red, there were large areas of dark blue and purple. The middle one, Hovda said, showed a comatose patient. The one on the left was the brain of a UCLA football player who had been injured in the first half of a game, went back to play the second half, and then walked into the emergency room the following day, complaining of a severe headache.

To Chiarelli, it was an epiphany.

"Those were the kids we were missing" in Iraq and Afghanistan, he said. "They'd go out and get concussed on a Tuesday, and they'd be out on patrol again on Thursday."

The military doctors had been willing to listen to Hovda's presentation when Chiarelli, who had four stars on his collar, asked them to attend the session. But when Chiarelli brought Hovda back to Washington to help develop a new protocol for treating service members exposed to blasts, the doctors insisted the military didn't need to change. Existing methods, they said, were fine.

Chiarelli was incensed. So, too, was General James Amos, then the second-in-command of the Marine Corps. He shared Chiarelli's view that more needed to be done to address mental health issues. At the first working session with Hovda and the doctors, the two generals had jumped out of their chairs. "We're going to bring some people in here who understand we've got a goddamned problem," Chiarelli huffed, before walking out of the room.

It wasn't going to be easy. And addressing battlefield concussions was only one of his challenges. He convened regular meetings to examine the case of every active-duty soldier who had committed suicide in the previous months. Were there warning signs? What should the Army have done differently? And he devoted hours each week to discussing post-traumatic stress. To dispel the stigma around it, he no longer referred to it as a disorder.

He learned that troops claiming post-traumatic stress—PTS, he insisted, not PTSD—were diagnosed with a twenty-question test. *Are you feeling irritable or having angry outbursts? Have you lost interest in things you used to enjoy?* There was no blood test or brain scan.

"Imagine going to your doctor because you think you have a broken leg and your doctor asks twenty questions, and then your doctor says, 'You don't have a broken leg. You can go home.' You'd say, 'Aren't you going to X-ray my leg?' That's how we diagnose PTS," he said. "This is like having a heart attack, and when you show up in a hospital, it's 1945."

Experts told him it would be years, if ever, before more advanced tests could be developed for PTS. So Chiarelli directed his energies toward expanding mental health treatment programs in war zones and on domestic bases, and he pushed military doctors to explore the efficacy of alternative therapies.

He achieved more headway in screening for traumatic brain injuries. In 2010, the Army and the Marine Corps developed a set of guidelines to follow after service members were exposed to a blast. If they were in a vehicle that was damaged by an explosion, or they were within fifty meters of a bomb detonation, or if they lost consciousness, they had to be given a thirty-question cognitive test. If they didn't get at least twenty-six questions correct, they were to be sent to a doctor for an evaluation. And even if they passed the cognitive test the first time, they were supposed to be reevaluated the following day.

"We had to ram it through the bureaucracy," Chiarelli said, but it was a rare victory in his fight with the doctors. They usually told him his ideas didn't make sense—politely, of course—or that they couldn't be implemented because of a lack of equipment or trained personnel. "It was a very frustrating experience," he recalled. "The system was very resistant to change."

Meanwhile, the number of suicides remained unacceptably high, and the PTSD/TBI bar on the graph continued to grow taller.

In January 2012, Chiarelli's term as vice-chief was over. That April, after nearly forty years in uniform, he retired.

He could have gone on to indulge his passion for golf or earn a hefty salary by working for a defense contractor, as many other retired generals have done. But Chiarelli couldn't walk away from PTS and TBI. There was nobody to pass his work on to, because no other four-star general shared his zeal to address those ailments. When he had been leading troops in a war zone, he had repeatedly told them that the Army would take care of them if they were hurt. He hadn't just been making speeches to prepare them for battle. He had been uttering a solemn promise, one that he was unwilling to walk away from, even in retirement.

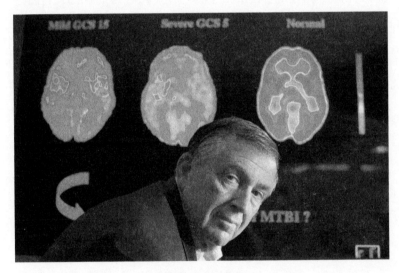

PETER CHIARELLI

Chiarelli moved back home to Seattle and assumed command of One Mind for Research, a nonprofit organization focused on advancing research and treatment of mental illness and brain injury. "I'm going to keep working this," he told friends in the Army. "I'm not throwing in the towel."

Chiarelli sought out the men and women he wanted to help by the dozens in military and Veterans Affairs hospitals. They were in pharmacies, seeking prescription refills. They were in outpatient clinics, waiting for a doctor to try out yet another "off label" drug on them—medicines originally developed to treat cancer, seizures, and other ailments that were being employed by desperate government physicians to address symptoms of PTS and TBI. And they were in the wards, hoping that one more MRI, one more rehabilitation therapy session, one more day away from the stresses of daily life, would ease their pain.

Marine corporal Chase Villavicencio was one of them. In 2011, he had tumbled off a ladder and struck his head as he tried to escape a Taliban mortar barrage in Afghanistan. Since then, he had suffered wrenching migraine headaches, bouts of dizziness, spells of intense anger, and memory loss. By late 2013, his forgetfulness had become apparent in his work as a radio-communications specialist. "I was making calls to the same person twice to set up appointments," he recalled. His superiors realized that he needed to get help, and in early 2014 they sent him to the VA hospital in Richmond, Virginia, where he met with one of the country's top TBI specialists in a laboratory filled with vials and beakers.

"When did you fall off the ladder?" asked David Cifu, the VA's national director of physical medicine and rehabilitation programs.

Villavicencio, a compact man, hunched over and began to count on his fingers.

"February, March, April," he whispered to himself as he pushed three fingers back.

"May," he said. "It was May of 2011."

He raised his head with an apologetic expression. "Sorry," he said. "Sometimes I have to count the months."

The old Villavicencio would have given the answer in an instant. "Simple things take me a while now," he said. "I have to concentrate. It doesn't come naturally anymore."

Cifu nodded understandingly. But he still needed details. The circumstances of Villavicencio's concussion were essential to determining whether he could be included in a first-of-a-kind study of the long-term effects of mild and moderate TBI.

"I remember hitting the ground," Villavicencio said.

"And then?" Cifu asked. "Were you awake?"

"I don't really remember."

"How long from la-la land to getting on your feet?"

"About an hour."

Villavicencio initially brushed off the fall, he said. Other Marines in the area had been shot. "My reaction was, 'I'm alive,' " he said. "I really didn't think much of it."

Then he started getting headaches. He couldn't stand bright sunlight. He developed a blurry spot when looking out of his right eye. He began to forget simple details. "All of a sudden I sound like an idiot," he said.

Still he didn't seek help. "In the Marine Corps, there's a mentality: there's a job to do," he said. "As long as you can keep moving, you keep moving."

As Villavicencio finished his story, Cifu explained why he was asking so many questions. He was leading a nationwide study that aimed to track two thousand veterans with moderate TBI for at least two decades. Would they develop early-onset Alzheimer's disease or other forms of dementia? Or would they bounce back? The sixty-two-million-dollar study, which was being paid for by the Pentagon and the VA, was among the initiatives Chiarelli had advocated for while he was vice-chief. Because of red tape and bickering among government officials, it had only gotten off the ground two years after he retired.

"We'd love to get you enrolled in this program," Cifu said to Villavicencio. He explained that participants would receive an annual brain MRI, extensive blood tests, and other assessments to monitor their recovery. "What you had was a concussion—no doubt about it," he said. "We're trying to better understand what happens to people who have concussions while at war."

Villavicencio looked intrigued. He had brought with him a copy of his favorite book, *The Road* by Cormac McCarthy. Once he had been able to zip through it. Now he read the lines over and over, struggling to grasp the meaning. He wondered if, one day, the words would become clearer. So did Cifu.

"We'd like to follow you for the rest of your life," the doctor said.

When Chiarelli retired, he thought he knew how to win the war against TBI and PTS. The problem, he assumed, was that research into those brain problems was underfunded. "I believed that if I used my good name, I could get money, and I could give it to researchers, and we'd be out of this in a few years," he said.

He wanted One Mind for Research to raise a half-billion dollars by the end of 2014, money that would be used to fund projects aimed at improving diagnoses and treatment. He began spending eight of every ten days on the road to meet with prospective donors—a far more grueling travel schedule than he had had as the Army's vice-chief. Along the way, he called upon the academic experts whom he hoped to fund. Learning about their work, he believed, would help him make a more compelling pitch to those writing the checks.

It also infuriated him. At a session with brain injury experts in Boston, one doctor told him that he had completed a study showing that a drug commonly used to treat TBI was ineffective and might actually be harming patients. *Holy shit,* Chiarelli thought.

"What's the drug?" he asked the doctor.

"I can't tell you that," the doctor replied.

"What do you mean?" Chiarelli responded.

The doctor told Chiarelli that a prestigious academic journal had agreed to publish his study in three months. He was prohibited from divulging the results until then.

"You mean we'll be giving people the wrong drug for three months?" an incredulous Chiarelli asked.

"Sir," the doctor said, "that's the way the system works."

The other physicians nodded understandingly at the doctor's explanation. "They all looked at me as if I had a third eye growing out of my head," Chiarelli said. "I was beside myself. When I was a general, if I had a defect on a helicopter and I waited three months to do anything—'Hey, check the torque or the bolts'—and another helicopter crashed, I'd be the subject of countless investigations."

Meetings with other academic researchers were less colorful but no less frustrating. Chiarelli discovered that they were collecting data on their subjects using different methods, making it difficult, if not impossible, to compare results. And he found that instead of collaborating, the smartest physicians and scientists were competing for the biggest share of a growing pot of federal research dollars. He had naively assumed that they would come together in the manner of the scientists who worked on the Manhattan Project to solve what he believed was a profound national challenge. Instead, they seemed to be acting as rainmakers for their universities. "They see data as their power to get more money," he said.

We have a totally dysfunctional research system, Chiarelli thought. *The problem isn't money. The problem is the doctors.* He tossed aside his fund-raising plan. "We've abdicated to the researchers," he said. "We're afraid to challenge them because they all went to school for twelve more years than we did."

Instead of accepting their way of doing business, or simply complaining about it to his military buddies at the officers' club, he decided to fight. He had been a four-star general, after all. He had run a war. He wasn't going to let petty rivalries and self-interest get in the way of helping veterans with PTS and TBI. He resolved that his organization would not "spend another cent on research" until he could find folks willing to work together.

Chiarelli figured he could get the federal government, which was spending tens of millions of dollars to bankroll most of the research, to help him out by requiring recipients of grants to collaborate. He made his case to the National Institutes of Health, the Department of Veterans Affairs, and his former colleagues in the Pentagon. They were polite but noncommittal.

A few months later, the NIH issued a grant for TBI research. It "highly encouraged" the winners to assemble data in a shareable way, but it did not require it. That wasn't good enough for Chiarelli. If the government wasn't going to take on the researchers, he'd do it himself.

It was a battle that came to consume almost every waking hour of his retired life. He no longer had hundreds of staff officers at his disposal, ready to execute orders; if he wanted something done, *he* had to do it. When he had to crisscross the country for meetings, as he did almost every week, he traveled in economy class, often on red-eyes. Gone were the days when he could summon one of the Army's executive jets.

Despite the relentless schedule, he carved out time to keep in touch with dozens of soldiers struggling with TBI and PTS whom he had met while he was in uniform. Among them was Major Ben Richards, who had suffered two concussions—one from a suicide bomb, the other from a roadside IED—while commanding an armored cavalry troop in Iraq. Upon his return, he had received his dream job in the Army—teaching history at West Point, his alma mater—but skull-splitting headaches, frequent insomnia, and flashes of anger rendered him unable to work. When doctors determined Richards's injuries were too significant to allow him to return to the classroom, Chiarelli promised to keep tabs on his recovery.

A few months later, when the general called, Richards was apoplectic. Military doctors had prescribed four drugs to help him with his symptoms. All of them were off-label; they hadn't been designed or tested for his ailments, but Army physicians determined they could nonetheless ease his suffering. And they did. His migraines subsided slightly. He was sleeping better. Then he went to the VA, which was responsible for his medical treatment once he retired from the Army.

The transition should have been a straightforward matter: transfer his files and continue his treatment. But the VA, as it does with all new veterans, insisted on conducting its own examinations and prescribing its own medicines. When Richards asked for refills of the four prescriptions that military doctors had so carefully calibrated for him, his VA doctor balked. The list of drugs VA physicians were authorized to prescribe, the doctor told him, was more limited than the military's, and two of the four medicines Richards was taking were not approved by the VA. When Richards warned that discontinuing one of them, a powerful drug intended to treat nerve pain, would subject him to severe withdrawal symptoms, the doctor still refused to budge. "We know this will put you in the emergency room," Richards remembers the doctor telling him.

Richards explained his predicament to Chiarelli, who became equally incensed. If the military deemed the drugs effective, he believed the VA had an obligation to provide them. This wasn't akin to substituting Advil for Tylenol. These medications, which were essential to helping severely injured veterans, couldn't be replaced with another bunch of pills. In between his work for One Mind, Chiarelli tried to bend as many ears as he could in Washington on the issue. But the VA refused to change its protocol, citing cost concerns.

How many veterans, Chiarelli wondered, wind up killing themselves because the medications they need aren't on the VA's list?

Richards dug into his savings and paid seventeen dollars a pill to slowly wean himself off the nerve-pain drug, but not every veteran can afford to do that.

On the Super Bowl Sunday after Chiarelli retired from the Army, the San Francisco 49ers squared off against the Baltimore Ravens. Instead of kicking back on his sofa with a cold beer and pretzels, Chiarelli spent the weekend at a meeting of brain specialists in Houston led by Geoffrey Manley, a neurosurgery professor at the University of California campus in San Francisco. Chiarelli regarded Manley, who had helped develop the new military concussion guidelines, as one of the smartest TBI specialists in the nation and a potential ally in promoting collaboration among researchers.

Manley had received a federal stimulus grant for a "shovel-ready project" to assess TBI patients as soon as they arrived in the emergency room and then track their recovery. The study collected patient information in an identical way at four different hospitals, allowing researchers to analyze and draw conclusions from a large pool of data. But the federal grant didn't include money to process the data. When Chiarelli learned about the shortfall in Houston, he saw an opportunity: he offered to have One Mind pick up the bill. Once the data were curated, Manley was elated. "This is amazing," he told Chiarelli.

As the two got to know each other, Chiarelli discovered that Manley shared many of his views about collaborative research. They discussed the unique national response to the AIDS crisis a generation earlier, when Congress funded public-private partnerships and top researchers agreed to work together to identify the virus and develop treatments. Those working on AIDS broke with protocol and shared their failures, not just successes, so others wouldn't pursue fruitless paths. "This is so stupid. What organization has a success like they did with AIDS and then doesn't change the way they do business?" Chiarelli said. "Why didn't they step back and say, 'This worked'? Instead, we went back to doing things the same old way."

Chiarelli saw TBI as a medical crisis as complicated and important as AIDS and knew that the fruits of the research would benefit not just veterans but car-crash victims, athletes, and millions of other people. An estimated three million Americans suffer head injuries every year, and it's the leading cause of death among adults between eighteen and forty-five. What was learned could also impact treatments for diseases such as Alzheimer's, Parkinson's, and amyotrophic lateral sclerosis. "You need the combined power of everyone working together," Chiarelli said.

A few months after the Houston meeting, when the National Institutes of Health announced an eighteen-million-dollar grant to conduct a larger version of Manley's initial study, Manley decided to give collaboration a shot. He assembled a team of ten other academic institutions to submit a joint application for the money. They offered to spread the work around the country, arguing that they would be able to assess a more diverse and representative sample of patients. Manley's team, which won the grant, also agreed to make its database publicly available six months after the study. Even though the work was not focused on veterans, Chiarelli was certain the findings would have a direct benefit to the military. "Anything more we learn about TBI helps."

As the study started, Chiarelli once again stepped in to finance what the government wouldn't. One Mind donated $500,000 to underwrite travel costs and stipends for victims to return to the hospital every few months so they could be tested. Although the alliance among the researchers remained fragile—some of their superiors wanted them to bid for the whole project by themselves—Chiarelli was overjoyed. "They're putting down their competitive instincts," he said of the researchers, "and working together for the good of the country."

But the fight was far from over. There still is not a reliable test to diagnose mild and moderate brain injuries, and treatment options remain woefully inadequate compared with advancements made over the past generation in cancer and heart-disease care. "We're basically treating these great volunteers the same way we treated their dads after Vietnam and their grandfathers after World War II," Chiarelli said. "We owe them more than that."

Every time he ran into an intransigent bureaucrat or an uncooperative researcher, he recalled the men and women who fought under his command in Iraq and those who came home racked by headaches, insomnia, anger, and blurry vision. He thought of warriors like Ben Richards, the West Point graduate who had been among the sharpest young men in the Army but was now homebound, incapacitated by migraines, consumed by rage, unable to concentrate enough to hold down a job.

And as Richards fought with the VA, he thought of Chiarelli, who went to war for guys like him every day. "We all talk about the warrior credo: 'Never leave a man behind.' But who actually lives that? He does," Richards said. "He could be living a comfortable life. There's no kudos for looking out for Ben Richards. But he does. Because he's one of the great heroes of our Army."

On a misty spring morning, Chiarelli walked into the lobby of the University of Pittsburgh's sports medicine center, past a row of autographed jerseys and helmets gifted by Steelers and Penguins players whose concussions had been treated within the modern, two-story building. He had come because he knew that professional football and ice hockey teams, whose trainers and coaches had once been as ignorant and inattentive to head injuries as the military, had begun to take these ailments more seriously. Among those at the vanguard of concussion research were specialists in Pittsburgh who cared for the city's elite athletes. Chiarelli wanted to know what they had learned.

"So many other places that you go to, people with TBI and concussions are sent home. 'Here's some pain meds. Rest for a few weeks in a dark room,'" he told the university doctors who sat across a table from him in a conference room. The doctors explained a new approach they had pioneered to assess the severity of a concussion through a four-minute physical examination, as well as a therapy that involved getting patients to quickly reengage their brains through complex movements and mental exercises. "We're convinced we can corner this injury," said Micky Collins, a University of Pittsburgh professor who ran the sports medicine center.

Chiarelli jotted copious notes on three-by-five index cards and then jumped in with questions: What about using MRIs to assess the severity of concussions? Is your test simple enough that military medics could give it while in the field? What links do you see between brain injuries and degenerative diseases such as Alzheimer's and Parkinson's?

"Dr. Chiarelli—" Collins said.

"I'm not a doctor."

"You sure sound like one."

Chiarelli spent the morning listening, questioning, observing. He accompanied Collins as he examined patients. Chiarelli stood off to the side, hands clasped in front, staring straight ahead. He toured the facility and struck up conversations with nurses in the hallways. He learned that specialists at the university had authored more than twenty academic papers on concussion diagnosis and treatment.

An hour later, over lunch at a seafood restaurant, Chiarelli told the doctors that the Pentagon had spent $700 million on traumatic brain injury research since 2002. "But do they have anything like this? No. I had the program for four years. Did I know any of this? No. I was going around talking about this for four fricking years, and did anyone ever tell me to come here? Here you guys are with a proven model, and here we are, in the military, limping along." He said their lessons needed to be shared with hospitals and rehabilitation centers across the country.

Collins said other experts were not yet willing to endorse their methods, which they were seeking to spread through articles in academic journals. "There's a lot of politics in this," he explained.

Chiarelli switched from listen mode to pitch mode. "Stop talking about twenty studies," he said. "Break through that. Let's move! We need action!"

As the day wore on, Chiarelli's excitement—and frustration—grew still more acute. One of the university's top neurosurgeons walked him through an ongoing, Pentagon-funded study to examine whether an expensive new brain-imaging tool, called high-definition fiber tracking, can more accurately diagnose TBI. Subjects in the study, most of whom were Iraq and Afghanistan veterans, spent three days receiving a comprehensive assessment. Before they went back home, they were given iPad tablets so they could take regular health surveys and video chat with doctors.

"Remarkable," Chiarelli gushed. "This has great promise."

Then he asked the neurosurgeon, David Okonkwo, whether he was collaborating with David Cifu, the VA doctor in Richmond who is leading the sixty-two-million-dollar longitudinal study.

"No," replied Okonkwo, who said the Defense Department, which funded both studies, did not require cooperation with other research projects.

"As a taxpayer, shouldn't I be pissed off as hell?" Chiarelli said. "What kind of system sets itself up like that?"

"I don't have a comeback for that," Okonkwo said.

Chiarelli slammed his hand on a stack of patient reports. "How long before this is ready for prime time?"

The surgeon warned Chiarelli not to expect immediate results. "I have a massive amount of respect for your impatience. But this isn't about flipping a switch or having a turnkey solution. It's about having people knowing what they're doing."

As Chiarelli rode to the airport in a taxi driven by a Vietnam veteran, the morning mist turned into the season's final snowfall. Chiarelli stared out at the white-flecked highway median. Then he looked at his itinerary. Washington next. Then Boston. More meetings, more researchers, more urgency.

CHAPTER TEN

I Miss You, Dad

Max Cabrera, a lanky, sandy-haired child, plopped onto the carpet of a meeting room at a Marriott hotel in Arlington, Virginia. For the past hour he had been fooling around with a Jenga game, trying to find other kids who could match his dexterity in removing rectangular wooden blocks from the base of a tower without toppling it. Now it was circle time. Two dozen children, all his age, and an equal number of adult mentors, most drawn from nearby military installations, sat together. The youngsters wore red T-shirts, the adults blue.

They passed a purple Nerf ball around counterclockwise. The person who held the ball introduced himself or herself while the others listened.

When the ball came to Max, he looked down.

"I am Max. I am nine years old. I lost my dad due to an explosion."

The ball moved along. Each time a kid held it, another snippet of heart-wrenching loss tumbled out.

My dad died when I was four weeks old—from a mine.

My daddy died from a bomb. He was an EOD tech. He defused one bomb, but there was another underneath.

My dad drowned in a tank.

My daddy died before I was born.

All of the children in the room had lost a parent who had been serving in the military. One perished in a training accident, another because of an illness. The rest died in Iraq and Afghanistan from IEDs and sniper fire, in helicopter crashes and tank rollovers.

Max was seven when his mother, August, brought him and his five-year-old brother, Roanin, into her room, sat them both on the bed, and held their hands. "Guys, I have something I need to tell you. There's been an accident. Daddy's been killed. He's not coming home."

Max collapsed.

Lieutenant Colonel David Cabrera had been traveling in an armored bus on Kabul's southern fringe, shuttling between two NATO bases, when a suicide bomber steering a car packed with explosives pulled up next to the bus and detonated. The force of the blast upended the shuttle and tossed it several yards. Dave and three other U.S. service members were killed.

August had waited three days to tell the boys. First, she had traveled to Dover Air Force Base in Delaware to sob at the sight of her husband's flag-draped casket, while the boys enjoyed a night of Halloween trick-or-treating. She consulted a book on talking to children about grieving. These sorts of hard conversations were something she always expected Dave to handle, not just because he was a good father, but because it was his job.

After earning a degree in psychology from Texas A&M University, Dave had joined the Army as a licensed clinical social worker. He wanted to see the world and help soldiers. He eventually earned a pediatric fellowship at a top military hospital and became one of the Army's most proficient counselors of grief-stricken children.

As the war in Iraq escalated, he deployed, spending five months tending to stressed-out, battle-scarred soldiers on forward operating bases. Upon his return, he became a casualty assistance officer, helping to care for families who had lost a relative in war. In 2010, he was appointed an assistant professor of family medicine at the Uniformed Services University of the Health Sciences, the Defense Department's in-house medical school. Although it was a dream job, allowing him to combine clinical work with research, he felt pulled by the war in Afghanistan. He hated to leave August and the boys, but there weren't enough social workers to meet the needs of soldiers on the war front. Even so, his Army superiors urged him to remain at the university, telling him he was too senior to go. Dave had to cajole half a dozen different officers to approve his deployment.

He arrived in Afghanistan on October 1, 2011. He was killed twenty-eight days later.

Dave's two young boys reacted to his death differently. Through two memorial services, a funeral, and the interment of Dave's ashes at Arlington National Cemetery, Roanin often screamed in anguish. Not Max. His mother was certain he was grieving, but he projected a stoicism beyond his years, rarely sobbing in the presence of others.

Once a week, August drove Max to a grief counselor, hoping that he'd open up about the loss of his father. After a few months, he told his mother, "I don't think I'm getting anything out of this."

"Why are we going?" she asked him.

"Well, I like the time with you in the car," he said. "And I like that he plays chess with me."

August discontinued the therapy. Max, she reasoned, could heal in his own way. But she didn't kid herself: he still had a giant hole in his heart. At night, Roanin, tucked into the lower half of the bunk bed they shared, would yell, "I miss Daddy. Why did he have to go?" Max would lie on the top bunk, crying quietly. "Big, silent tears," August said, "that just break your heart."

August, a petite brunette who had met Dave at a costume party ten years earlier and decided on the spot that she was going to marry him, tried to hold herself together for the boys. Friends and family swooped in to help. She busied herself by planning to move the family back to Washington State. But some nights, after the kids fell asleep, she'd curl up on her cold kitchen floor and sob uncontrollably.

Dave, why did you leave? Why me? Why us? These kids don't deserve this.

One night, as the tears rolled down her cheeks, her eyes fell on a white teardrop-shaped stress ball on the windowsill over the sink. The ball had arrived in a package soon after Dave's death, along with a coffee mug, a candle, a benefits guide for survivors, and a picture book about Klinger, a young horse that is overcome with sadness when he must leave his parents but finds fulfillment as a member of the caisson platoon at Arlington National Cemetery. The box was sent by TAPS, the Tragedy Assistance Program for Survivors. When it had come, August didn't bother to read any of the literature. She gave the book to the kids, put the mug in the dishwasher, and set the ball next to the window. But now, as she gazed at the teardrop, she saw that a toll-free phone number was printed on it.

"So I called them, hysterical," she recalled. "And somebody answered the phone and let me talk. She said, 'We're here. You can call anytime.'"

August soon learned that every year on Memorial Day weekend, TAPS hosts a national military survivor seminar in Arlington. Hundreds of widows and a few widowers attend, as well as parents, siblings, and grandparents. There are practical sessions with titles like "Proactive Grieving," "Healing for Suicide Survivors," and "Your Family's Financial Future." And there are fun sessions, too, devoted to indoor rock climbing, kayaking, and gentle yoga.

While the adults meet, kids attend their own program. TAPS calls it the Good Grief Camp. In May 2014, five hundred children filled a hotel ballroom. The sea of red-shirted campers, ranging from angelic-looking kindergartners to sullen high schoolers, is almost as breath-stopping a sight as Section 60 in Arlington, the final home for many of their parents.

August brought Max and Roanin and invited Dave's two children with his first wife, Corbin and Gillian, who live in Abilene, Texas. Sixteen-year-old Corbin flew in, but his sister, who is a year younger, had to stay home for a dance recital.

Each child is paired with a mentor, almost all of whom are members of the military in their twenties and thirties stationed at the Pentagon and bases in the Washington area. They devote an entire holiday weekend to amusing, comforting, and supervising their charges. The mentors' name tags are festooned with colored ribbons that indicate their service—Army, Navy, Marines, or Air Force—and organizers seek to match them with kids whose deceased parent served in the same branch.

Max, however, was among thirty campers whose mentors wore a white ribbon, denoting a different qualification for volunteering at the camp. Like the kids to whom these adults were assigned, they were survivors.

Max's mentor, a stocky young man with a close-cropped beard and wire-rimmed glasses, introduced himself right after Max spoke in the circle.

"Hi, I'm Beau Dolan. I lost my father when I was y'all's age. I was nine. I was in this group thirteen years ago."

His father, Captain Robert E. Dolan, had been skippering a remarkable career. A Naval Academy graduate, he had been given command of an eight-thousand-ton destroyer when he was just forty. Then he received a prestigious Pentagon assignment as head of the Navy's strategy and concepts branch. He was in his office on the first floor of the building's D Ring on the morning of September 11, 2001. He never returned home.

Beau grieved as Max does. He was a shy boy who found unsettling the attention lavished upon him by family and friends, and by a nation reeling from the terrorist attacks. At his elementary school, he was an object of sympathy and fascination. None of the other kids had lost a parent in the Pentagon.

The following May, Beau's mother brought him and his sister to the TAPS camp so they could grieve with other military children and spend a weekend not being "the kid who lost his dad on 9/11." Beau arrived petrified. He enjoyed playing chess—his father had taught him—and reading, not running amok in a hotel, jumping into games of tag and dodgeball. But sharing memories of his father proved cathartic, as did touristy excursions with the other kids to the National Zoo, the Smithsonian museums, and the monuments on the Mall.

He came back the next year and the year after. Then he was done. He still grieved, but he didn't want his survivor status to define his life. He channeled his energies into studying and playing football. He believed his father was looking down from heaven, and sought to make him proud. He finished high school and attended Notre Dame.

The week after his college graduation, Beau could have traveled to Texas to hang out with his girlfriend or simply have slept, which was tempting after his twelve-hour drive home to Alexandria, Virginia, from South Bend, Indiana. Instead, he came to camp.

"It's a pay-it-forward kind of deal," he said. "I went through it, and I'd like to help other kids who are going through what I had to deal with at that age."

And so the twenty-two-year-old found himself in Salon J of the Crystal Gateway Marriott, surrounded by two dozen nine- and ten-year-olds, several of whom were pelting balls at each other. To Beau's relief, Max didn't join in, preferring to fiddle with his wooden Jenga blocks.

After the introductory circle, campers and mentors were asked to draw a picture of what they imagined their loved one was doing at that moment. Max scribbled Dave, up in the clouds, playing with their dog, Sinjin. Beau drew his dad in the clouds as well, playing chess, also with the family dog.

"Do you think your dad is with the apostles now?" Beau asked Max.

"Yeah."

"I think my dad is, too."

The Good Grief Camp owes its existence to three gray whales who became trapped in a polar ice pack near Point Barrow, Alaska, in 1988. After the whales' plight made national news, President Ronald Reagan asked one of his West Wing aides, Bonnie Mersinger, to contact the Alaska National Guard and offer federal assistance. She tracked down the man heading the rescue operation, Colonel Tom Carroll. They talked and talked and fell in love as two of the whales were freed. After Reagan left the White House, Bonnie married Tom and moved to Alaska. He became a one-star general and the commander of the state's Army National Guard. That was how Hollywood ended the story—depicted in the movie *Big Miracle,* starring Drew Barrymore—but Bonnie's real life soon descended into Greek tragedy. In November 1992, after they had been married just three years, Tom's National Guard plane slammed into a mountain on an approach to Juneau.

Bonnie Carroll felt as if her life had stopped. She had trouble breathing. When she went outside, it seemed odd that stores were open and that other people were going about their business as if

nothing were amiss. She wanted to scream out the lines of W. H.
Auden's famous poem to passersby:

Stop all the clocks, cut off the telephone,
Prevent the dog from barking with a juicy bone,
Silence the pianos and with muffled drum
Bring out the coffin, let the mourners come.

After several weeks, Bonnie decided that it might help to com-
miserate with others who had lost a spouse in similar circumstances.
She sat with support groups for wives of police officers killed in the
line of duty, victims of violent crime, and people who had relatives
in hospice care. At each meeting, she had the same reaction: *I don't
fit in.*

The following Memorial Day, at a ceremony to honor the
Guardsmen who had been on Tom's plane, Bonnie met the other
grieving families. After the service, they all gathered for coffee at
a nearby restaurant. Their conversations about their loved ones,
their grief, and their worries for the future led into lunch and then
stretched to dinner. From that day forward, the families stayed connected, hanging out at each other's houses and even vacationing
together. "We just formed this really tight bubble," Bonnie recalled.
"We could laugh. We could cry. We could say things that nobody
else could understand."

Over the year that followed, she sought to reach out to a larger
support network of military survivors, joining the Gold Star Wives
of America and the Society of Military Widows. But those groups
were focused on advocating for government benefits for survivors
and organizing social activities, not on talking about pain, crying
on each other's shoulders, or doling out loving hugs. Bonnie, who
began to split her time between Alaska and the Washington, D.C.,
area, asked friends in the Pentagon and others who were connected

to the military, Where can I find a support group for people like me? Nobody had an answer.

Bonnie decided to start her own. To her, TAPS wasn't just a cute acronym. She wasn't going to duplicate the services provided by the military immediately after a service member died. Her group would focus instead on the needs of families in the painful months and years after the final rendition of taps at their loved one's funeral. On the model of Alcoholics Anonymous, it would be peer to peer. "When it comes to grief and traumatic loss, it's not a mental ill-ness," Bonnie said. "It is not a physical injury. You really can't take a pill to get better or get over it. But what you can do is connect with another who has walked that journey."

Her first seminar, held in Arlington in 1995, drew a few dozen spouses and a handful of kids, all of whom had lost loved ones in training accidents or plane crashes, or to illness. The organization grew slowly. Then came September 11, 2001.

Bonnie, who combines Energizer Bunny stamina with bottom-less empathy, put out a call to all of the group's volunteer mentors. A dozen arrived within a day, and a similar number would show up every week for the next six weeks. That participation earned imme-diate credibility with the Defense Department: TAPS became the only nongovernmental organization other than the Red Cross to be allowed inside the hotel that housed the military's assistance center for Pentagon victims' families.

The next year, the seminar swelled with 9/11 families, including Beau Dolan, his sister, and their mother. Then came the start of the Iraq war. Bonnie was forced to move the event to a larger venue. In 2014, twenty-four hundred participants spilled across two hotels. In between the annual seminar and camp, TAPS hosts sixty other events, including gatherings for suicide survivors, retreats for par-ents, and camping trips.

Bonnie wore a button that proclaimed "I'm a hugger," and she lived up to it. As she walked down the halls, every second person received an embrace. "It's powerful to know that you're not alone, to know that there are others who have felt this pain and have survived it."

The second night of camp, after eating Domino's pizza on the National Mall, running through an obstacle course organized by National Football League players, feeding handfuls of grass to U.S. Park Police horses, watching the Air Force drill team do some routines, and spending four hours wandering through the zoo, Beau and Max headed to the District of Columbia's Armory, a cavernous, timeworn arena that TAPS had transformed into a fantasyland. There were half a dozen enormous inflated bounce houses, a rock-

BEAU DOLAN HOLDS MAX CABRERA

climbing wall, a laser-tag room, and face-painting and cupcake-decorating stations. Buffalo Wild Wings and Panda Express provided dinner.

Grief was checked at the door. Here, there were no circles for remembering loved ones, no drawing exercises, no dance therapy sessions. It was just fun. And Max had plenty of it.

He challenged Beau to a race through the most difficult inflatable structure. Max bounded out first. Beau followed him, winded. "I guess you can tell," he said with a sigh to another mentor, "that I'm one of the few nonmilitary people here." Max didn't mind. He thought it was cool that his mentor had a special connection with him, that he knew what it feels like to have your dad snatched from you.

In Beau's eyes, Max wasn't just a survivor. Beau saw his younger self reflected in Max's reticence, his love of board games, his recall of random trivia. He sensed that Max related to the camp the same way he had: it was less a forum for outward displays of emotion or public healing than a weekend when he could just feel normal again.

"It's not like losing a cat or a dog, even though dogs are really close to people," Max said. His friends back home "don't know what it feels like to lose someone close."

Earlier that day, as Max and Beau had worked to design a chessboard out of construction paper and crayons in homage to their fathers, the half generation that divided them had seemed to melt away. But on the bus to the zoo, Beau was reminded of how much did separate them. Beau had remarked to Max that he often traveled by bus when he was younger.

Why didn't you fly? Max asked.

Beau said he didn't fly until he was sixteen. His mother still hated to fly.

Why, Beau?

"Remember September 11?" he replied. "There was a terrorist attack. Terrorists flew a plane into the Pentagon. My dad was in it. Ever since, my mom has been scared of planes."

Max's eyes widened.

"It was in 2001," Beau explained. "Before you were born."

Beau told him about the worst day of his life. "They captured the pilots and took over the planes." He described the attack on the World Trade Center, the hijackers' allegiance to Osama bin Laden and al-Qaeda.

"What they believed was really hateful," he said. "They thought they'd be rewarded when they died."

Max nodded. He knew that a suicide attacker had killed his dad, too. His mom had told him. A few months after Dave's death, she had urged him not to be angry with his father's killer. "He probably got told things like if he does this, he'll get to heaven. If he does this, his family will be saved. If he does this, it's a good thing. He was fed lies his whole life. They don't know the truth, so we can't be angry at him for believing lies. We have to pray for him. Being angry at the bomber isn't going to solve anything."

Max repeated none of that to Beau. He gazed out the window as the bus pulled into the zoo.

On the camp's third and final day, the kids were given squares of paper and asked to write notes to their loved ones. The notes would be attached to red, white, and blue helium balloons that the campers would release into the air next to the Pentagon.

I love you, Dad, Max wrote. *Please help all of us to be better people in life, like you.*

Beau wrote one too.

I miss you. I wish you could see all the changes in my life . . .

Beau wished his father could have been in South Bend a week

earlier, as he accepted his diploma. The toughest moments were life's milestones, when he'd look out at the crowd and wish his dad were in it. He knew Max would feel that same pain in the coming years.

Before departing, the campers and the mentors gathered in another circle. The lights in the room were dimmed, and each survivor was given a paper bag containing a battery-operated candle. Each of them, in turn, placed the glowing bag in the center of the circle, announcing the person it was commemorating.

I'm here for my daddy.

I'm here for my father.

I'm here for my dad. I miss you so much.

I'm here for my dad, Lieutenant Colonel David Cabrera.

I'm here for my dad, Captain Bob Dolan.

When Beau rejoined the circle after setting down his lantern, he rested his hand on Max's back. The two of them stared at the lights flickering through star-shaped cutouts. In that moment, they weren't mentor and camper, college graduate and elementary school kid. The years between them vanished. They were two sons missing their dads.

Epilogue

So many of the men and women in this book committed extraordinary acts of valor. So, too, did hundreds of others among the 2.6 million Americans who served in Iraq and Afghanistan. To the generals who led the wars, it seemed that every week, sometimes every day, yielded another account of remarkable courage.

In an era when the work ethic and collective spirit of young adults have been called into question, we cannot ignore how many of them stepped up in a moment of need; how professionally, selflessly, and honorably they performed their duties; and how often they risked their lives to save their comrades. Their character deserves to be celebrated with the same pride the nation shows for the World War II veterans.

Many post-9/11 service members have been presented with medals, but a tally of metal and ribbon cannot capture the full extent of battlefield heroism. As most who have served in the wars will attest, they witnessed moments of spectacular bravery, compassion, and patriotism that never got written up for broader recognition. They remain known only to the men and women who were there.

Even when awards are presented, who pays attention anymore? Medal ceremonies, even those at the White House, barely attract a mention in the media. During the 1940s, the government paraded Medal of Honor recipients around the country to encourage people to purchase war bonds. Today, the awardees melt back into society. That's fine with them, of course. They hardly did what they did for fame.

But we owe it to them, and to ourselves, to understand what they did. That's why we profiled Leroy Petry, Kyle White, Bill Krissoff, Kellie McCoy, Jordan Haerter, Jonathan Yale, and the Ranger platoon. We believe their stories, and those of many others who participated in the wars, must be woven into our collective national narrative.

Our inattention to the wars doesn't just give short shrift to heroes. It harms everyone who served. In a society in which, as we've said, less than 1 percent join the military, and only about 5 percent have an immediate family connection to someone who fought in the Iraq and Afghanistan wars, the other 95 percent have an obligation to understand who their warriors are, what they've done, and what they can yet accomplish.

Our forebears knew. Their fathers, sons, and brothers served in the military, as did their neighbors. Even if returning troops didn't want to share their war stories over the dinner table, even if they had nightmares or needed to drink with their buddies once a week at the VFW hall, Americans back then knew that veterans had something valuable to offer the nation upon their return, and they knew that most could and would overcome the horrors of combat—because they knew their veterans.

But that tie is no more. Today's all-volunteer military doesn't spread the burden of warfare across society. It lays that burden on a fraction of our population, and those families often live on walled-off bases, cut off from the very citizens they have vowed to protect.

With so few possessing a direct link to someone who has served in Iraq or Afghanistan, many Americans don't understand that most of our veterans are not damaged, and even those suffering from trauma or physical injuries can have an enormously positive impact in their communities. They don't realize that our veterans can make—and are making—valuable contributions in the worlds of business, government, education, public health, and community service.

This division also leads veterans to undervalue their own potential. "Because there wasn't a draft, they weren't serving next to pharmacists and car repair shop owners and artists and teachers and journalists and business owners," said Eric Greitens, a former Navy SEAL who founded The Mission Continues, which offers veterans six-month fellowships to volunteer at nonprofit organizations. "They were serving with other people who had served in the military, and so what that meant was they have a far more limited conception of what they can do in the outside world when they get out. They think too often that because I know how to use a gun, maybe I can be a security guard."

Some returning warriors have begun to plow their leadership skills and commitment to serve into initiatives to strengthen and rebuild our country. Consider Greg Behrman, a naval intelligence officer who served in Afghanistan. Upon arriving home in Connecticut, he discovered that despite grand commitments in Washington to end veteran homelessness, many former service members in his state were living in alleys, cars, and parks. To tackle the problem, he formed a nonprofit organization called the Connecticut Heroes Project and set out to improve collaboration among federal and state agencies and private social-service organizations. And when, in the summer of 2014, he met Vietnam-era veteran George Martin on a park bench in New Haven because government paperwork delays were preventing him from moving into an apartment, Behrman withdrew cash from his own checking account and rented Martin a motel room for a week. "It's really cool," Martin said, "that you young veterans are looking out for old guys like me."

Veterans across the nation are engaging in similar selfless acts every day. That's why we profiled Team Rubicon, David Oclander, and Pete Chiarelli.

The post-9/11 years have brought us the longest period of sustained warfare in our nation's history. We have met this unprecedented challenge with a small cadre of citizens who charged forth to serve so that the rest of us could go on with life as usual. We have asked so much of them—and their families. The multiple, yearlong deployments that many uncomplainingly fulfilled often amounted to more time on the battlefield than their parents faced in Vietnam or their grandparents confronted in World War II. They missed birthdays and graduations, dance recitals, and Little League games. Many spent their tours in Iraq and Afghanistan under the constant threat of getting blown up. And yet we have sacrificed so little. In nonmilitary families, fathers could play catch with their sons, and wives could dine with their husbands, whenever they wanted; mothers didn't have to spend sleepless nights wondering if their adult children would return home alive.

For too long, too many of us have paid scant attention to the commitment of a brave few in our midst. It is unhealthy for a nation to become detached from those who secure it. Our volunteers have given the rest of us a remarkable freedom, but that freedom comes with the responsibility to understand their sacrifice, to honor them, to appreciate what they can offer when they return home, to care for those who are wounded, and to mourn those who have given us their last full measure of devotion.

As the war in Afghanistan winds down, it is tempting to see this as a moot issue. It is not. Our nation will continue to send men and women into harm's way for years to come, albeit in smaller tranches, as extremists bent on attacking the United States and our citizens abroad find safe haven in lawless parts of the Middle East and Africa. But the next phase of our wars is shifting to the home front. More than 1.5 million post-9/11 veterans have already taken off their uniforms and entered the civilian world. Another million will be following them in the next few years, as enlistments end and budget cuts shrink our military. They deserve to enter a society that welcomes them with an appreciation and understanding of their sacrifice.

If you are among those Americans with no direct connection to someone who has served in Iraq or Afghanistan, you can start to learn about those who safeguard us. If you encounter a veteran, say something more than "Thank you for your service." Ask a thoughtful question or two—and listen to his or her story. Many veterans are eager to explain how they served and what they're doing now. Meet their spouses and discover how strong and resilient they are.

Not all veterans will want to discuss their combat experiences. If they're reticent, don't push them. Our veterans aren't yearning for a ticker-tape parade. They just want their fellow citizens to care about what they did. The landmark *Washington Post*–Kaiser poll of post-9/11 veterans found that four in ten of them feel civilians are "just saying what people want to hear" when they express their appreciation. In part, that's because the public expressions of thanks have become rote. Our interest in our veterans must be genuine, and so should our gratitude.

If listening and learning motivate you to take action, seek out a veterans' organization in your community. If you emerge impressed, volunteer your time or offer a modest donation. Or attend one of their events. Show up at the barbecue or the pancake breakfast. Meaningful engagement doesn't require lots of time or money.

If you are an employer, give veterans a fair shake. They don't want your pity or a handout. What they deserve, however, is genuine understanding and appreciation of the skills they've gleaned.

Serving in the military qualifies one to be more than a security guard. Veterans come with a can-do spirit. Many possess leadership and decision-making experiences that exceed that of civilians two decades their senior. They know how to follow orders but also how to exercise initiative. Hiring veterans isn't charity—it's good business.

If you are an elected official, forgo partisan bickering on veterans' issues. These men and women need our nation's leaders to come together, regardless of political stripe, and fulfill our obligations to them. They deserve a Congress that can find common ground on veterans' issues and craft productive legislation. They deserve a Department of Veterans Affairs that promptly and courteously provides them with top-quality health care and supplies compensation for injuries without delay.

If you are a veteran, don't underestimate yourself, and don't give up when you encounter obstacles along the way. As many of you know—and others will soon discover—the transition into civilian life isn't easy. Unlike the Greatest Generation, which entered an American economy with plenty of manufacturing jobs, the opportunities that await you require education and specialized skills.

Avail yourself of the post-9/11 GI Bill benefits, the most generous federal education support for veterans in our nation's history. And follow the example of Kyle White—not what he did on the hills of eastern Afghanistan, but after he got out of the Army: Instead of using his GI Bill to take easy classes in college, he challenged himself by taking math courses so he could graduate with a degree in business administration. Now he has a good-paying job as an investment analyst. "I couldn't rest on what I did out there on the mountain," he said. "We veterans have been given great opportunities—we just have to seize them."

=★=

The effort to bridge the civilian-military divide doesn't take much—just a little curiosity and a willingness to reach out.

Christopher Bridner, a twenty-six-year-old who works in corporate finance, grew up near Baltimore not knowing anyone, save for his grandfather, who had been in the military. He hadn't paid much attention to the wars in Iraq and Afghanistan, but he assumed most veterans were saddled with severe post-traumatic stress.

Soon after Navy SEALs killed Osama bin Laden in 2011, Bridner saw a video clip of Naval Academy midshipmen celebrating as the news broke. Led by the school's commandant speaking through a bullhorn, the students amended their traditional chant of "I believe that we will win" to a collective shout of "I believe that we have won!" Bridner, sitting in his office cubicle, got chills. Then he asked himself, *What am I actually doing to support them?*

He wrote small checks to the Navy SEAL Foundation and the Green Beret Foundation. Then he joined a group of flag-waving volunteers at Baltimore/Washington International Airport to welcome home a planeload of troops from Afghanistan. But he never got a chance to talk to any of them; they were rushing off to meet family or hop onto connecting flights.

Sometime later, he logged on to Facebook and saw that a coworker had posted a link to photographs of a man who was marching a hundred miles in near-freezing weather to raise money for wounded troops. Bridner decided to donate to the cause and began to follow the man's journey. The next day, the man posted a photograph of two men bringing him new boots. They were wearing shirts bearing the words "Team Red, White, and Blue." Bridner grew curious.

He discovered that the group—members refer to it as Team RWB—began by organizing fitness activities for veterans in cities across the United States. But in 2013, its founder, Mike Erwin, a major in the Army, decided to encourage civilians to join RWB's ranks. He wanted to provide them with "a chance not just to thank veterans for their service, but to get to know us." And, he figured, getting to know civilians could help many veterans as they transitioned out of the military bubble.

To Bridner, a trim type 1 diabetic who exercises regularly to regulate his blood sugar, the group seemed particularly interesting. He worried that he wouldn't have much to discuss with men and women who had been to war, but he figured he'd give it a try. The next week, he left work early on a Wednesday to join an RWB chapter in Montgomery County, Maryland, for a three-mile evening run.

As the group set out, he chatted with other runners about fitness regimens and plans for the upcoming weekend. He had no idea who was a veteran and who wasn't—everyone wore identical red RWB shirts—but it didn't matter. They were just a group of men and women, in their twenties and thirties, getting exercise and having a good time.

After the run, they all repaired to a Mexican restaurant. Bridner sat next to Steven Lim, an Army captain who had served two tours in Iraq and one in Kuwait. They began talking about football: Bridner is an ardent Baltimore Ravens fan, while Lim, who grew up in northern Virginia, is partial to the Washington Redskins. The conversation eventually shifted to more serious topics. Lim, who was preparing to leave the military after twelve years in uniform, was anxious about finding a job. Bridner offered advice about job hunting.

Lim had never expected a civilian would care enough to help. And Bridner had figured the veterans wouldn't want to talk to him because he hadn't served. Instead, he discovered that "they were just as welcoming to me as someone they literally fought side by side with."

He showed up the following Wednesday and every week thereafter. His colleagues knew why he slipped out early. "Running with your veterans' group," they'd say. But Bridner didn't think of it that way. *I'm running with my friends.*

In October 1945, *The Saturday Evening Post* published an issue with a Norman Rockwell painting titled *Homecoming Marine* on its cover. It depicts a young Marine in his service khakis, a Silver Star ribbon affixed to his chest, holding a Japanese flag as he sits on a box in a garage. He is talking to four men and two boys, all of whom are paying rapt attention.

General Martin Dempsey, the nation's top military officer, keeps a replica of that painting in his office. If Rockwell were to have illustrated a Marine returning from Vietnam, Dempsey said, he would have had to show a crowd turning away. And if he had been alive to capture a Marine upon his return from Afghanistan or Iraq, he likely would have portrayed people too caught up in their lives to listen to the veteran's story. "We need the image of our returning veterans to look more like this," Dempsey said, placing his hands on the old painting. "They are to be admired because they chose to live an uncommon life in service of their country."

The challenge is upon us. This is the time to start bridging the civilian-military divide. This is the moment to demonstrate our collective potential to come together and do right by those who have done so much for us.

They stepped up. Now it's our turn.

For a list of the charities supported with proceeds from this book, and for additional resources to learn about and engage with our veterans, please visit:

www.forloveofcountrybook.com

Acknowledgments

We are in debt to the 2.6 million American volunteers who deployed to Iraq, Afghanistan, and elsewhere in the world in support of those wars. Perhaps the most difficult aspect of writing this book was selecting whom to profile. We found remarkable stories from the war fronts, on the home front, everywhere we looked. We are deeply grateful for our subjects' willingness to devote days and sometimes weeks to opening their lives to us, to share sometimes painful memories, and to introduce us to their comrades-in-arms. The more time we spent with them, the more impressed—and humbled—we came to feel.

Bob Gates was a source of inspiration and wise counsel throughout this project, helping us to understand the profound contributions our service members make while deployed and what they can offer our society as veterans. Pete Chiarelli was another sage mentor, as was Leroy Petry, who showed just how humble and full of humor our heroes can be. Bill "Coach" Campbell started this journey by inviting Howard to speak at West Point in 2011.

Martin Dempsey, the chairman of the Joint Chiefs of Staff, was generous with his time. His director of warrior and family support, Jim Isenhower, helped us navigate the military bureaucracy to arrange interviews and obtain documents.

Several senior military officers provided valuable insights and offered crucial assistance: Jim Amos, Ken Dahl, Joe Dunford, Pat Ellis, John Kelly, Scott Miller, Rich Mills, and Larry Nicholson. Thanks also to Steve Lanza and other commanders at Joint Base Lewis-McChord for their support.

We would like to express our appreciation to the many military public affairs personnel who helped us along the way. At the Seventy-Fifth Ranger Regiment: Tracy Bailey, Brian DeSantis, and Michael Noggle. At the Tenth Mountain Division headquarters in Afghanistan: Loran Doane, Kap Kim, and Tage Rainsford. At the Pentagon: Alayne Conway, John Kirby, Elissa Smith, Ed Thomas, and Steve Warren. In Charlotte: Craig Norton.

We also benefited from conversations with leaders and members of nonprofit organizations that work tirelessly to improve the lives of veterans and their families. Among those that provided extraordinary assistance was Rally Point/6 in Lakewood, Washington, which opened its doors to our team.

At Starbucks, Howard has been fortunate to work with many partners who have served in the military. Its employee group, the Starbucks Armed Forces Network, anchored by Mick James and Rob Porcarelli, brought Leroy Petry to speak to the company's leaders, an event that provided the impetus for this book. We are grateful for the wise contributions from many on the Starbucks team, including Troy Alstead, Virginia Bergin, Cliff Burrows, John Culver, Corey duBrowa, John Kelly, Blair Taylor, and Gina Woods. Tim Donlan, Nancy Kent, Jonathan Nedved, and Carol Sharp provided key logistical assistance. Howard is also thankful for the support and enthusiasm of the Starbucks board of directors. Thanks as well to Placido Arango, Zoë Baird, Alan Cohen, Nicole David, Bill Etkin, Steve Fleischmann, Mesh Gelman, Tal Hirshberg, Erik Hyman, Bobby Kotick, Tony La Russa, Dan Levitan, Doron Linz, Max Mutchnick, Walter Robb, Faiza Saeed, Suzanne Sullivan, Richard Tait, and John Yamin.

We are very grateful for our friendship with Richard Plepler, the chairman and chief executive of HBO, and Jamie Dimon, the chairman and chief executive of JPMorgan Chase, who have been key partners in helping to spread the message of this book. And a special thank you to David Geffen and Jimmy Iovine for all their support and friendship.

The poll of Iraq and Afghanistan veterans conducted by *The Washington Post* and the Kaiser Family Foundation deepened our understanding of the challenges facing returning service members and helped to propel this project. The poll was conceived and conducted by Mollyann Brodie, Scott Clement, Jon Cohen, Peyton Craighill, and Claudia Deane.

Rajiv has been fortunate to work with some of the world's best journalists at the *Post*. He is grateful for the support of Katharine Weymouth, Marty Baron, Cameron Barr, Tim Curran, David Finkel, Peter Finn, Anne Kornblut, Carlos Lozada, Jason Ukman, and Scott Wilson.

Rafe Sagalyn deftly turned the idea for this book into a real ink-on-paper production, offering warm friendship and good humor at every step. We also appreciate the diligence of John DeLaney at ICM Partners.

Pulling this book together would not have been possible without the brilliant work of researchers Eve Hunter and Julie Tate. Sarah Courteau, one of the most talented editors in the country, sharpened almost every line. We were also helped by Maryanne Warrick, Michel duCille, and Pat Wingert Kelly.

The team at Knopf, led by Sonny Mehta, proved once again that they are the best in the publishing business. Jon Segal, who edited Rajiv's two previous books, was an invaluable partner, wielding his pen to make every paragraph smarter and clearer. Many others at Knopf rowed hard to get this book launched effectively, especially Paul Bogaards, Erinn Hartman, Brittany Morrongiello, and

Meghan Houser. Special thanks to production editor Maria Massey, who changed her summer vacation plans to work on the manuscript.

We want to single out for particular recognition two men who have been essential to every step of this project, offering priceless guidance and feedback: Daniel Pitasky, the executive director of the Schultz Family Foundation, and Vivek Varma, Starbucks' executive vice president of public affairs. We became collaborators through Vivek, who has been friends with Rajiv for fifteen years.

The other key partners in this venture were our families, whose love and support encouraged us forward.

Howard: My wife, Sheri, and our children, Jordan and Addison, created the Schultz Family Foundation with me, and along with my daughter-in-law, Breanna, they share my passion for supporting our veterans. Sheri has joined me in this project from the beginning, accompanying me on visits to military installations and in meetings with veterans. She is a stalwart advocate for ensuring that those who have served our nation in uniform have a successful transition to civilian life.

Rajiv: My parents, Uma and Kumar, and in-laws, Ellen and Seymour, helped to care for my two adorable sons, Max and Leo, during my long nights at work and frequent reporting trips. But nobody shouldered a greater burden than my wife, Julie, who juggled running a business with raising two young kids as I hunched over my keyboard. She never complained. "When I think about how tough it is when you go away for a week, I think of the wives whose husbands are in Afghanistan for a year," she told me once. "It puts it all into perspective."

ILLUSTRATION CREDITS ★

PAGE 29. Courtesy of Bill Krissoff

PAGE 40. Department of the Army

PAGE 59. Master Sergeant Kap Kim, Department of Defense

PAGE 77. Courtesy of Rebecca Yale (Yale) and JoAnn Lyles (Haerter)

PAGE 101. Courtesy of Linda Ferrara

PAGE 118. Michel duCille

PAGE 137. Courtesy of Kirk Jackson

PAGE 158. Michel duCille

PAGE 169. Michel duCille

PAGE 191. Rajiv Chandrasekaran